forever
skills

forever
skills

forever skills

THE 12 SKILLS TO FUTURE PROOF YOURSELF, YOUR TEAM AND YOUR KIDS

KIERAN FLANAGAN + DAN GREGORY

WILEY

First published in 2019 by John Wiley & Sons Australia, Ltd
42 McDougall St, Milton Qld 4064

Office also in Melbourne

Typeset in 11.5/14pt Adobe Garamond Pro

© John Wiley & Sons Australia, Ltd 2019

The moral rights of the authors have been asserted

 A catalogue record for this book is available from the National Library of Australia

Cover design and front cover image (infinity symbol): The Impossible Institute

Front cover image (pen): © NewFabrika/Shutterstock-pen

Back cover photo: © Oli Sansom

Printed in the United States of America by Quad/Graphics.

V6BB57AC6-17BE-4F84-9AD3-E7783F57EBF6_081919

Disclaimer

The material in this publication is of the nature of general comment only, and does not represent professional advice. It is not intended to provide specific guidance for particular circumstances and it should not be relied on as the basis for any decision to take action or not take action on any matter which it covers. Readers should obtain professional advice where appropriate, before making any such decision. To the maximum extent permitted by law, the authors and publisher disclaim all responsibility and liability to any person, arising directly or indirectly from any person taking or not taking action based on the information in this publication.

*To Gary and Darcy, my forever people,
and to Kerryanne, for being forever in my corner.*

CONTENTS

CONTENTS

ACKNOWLEDGEMENTS

'If I have seen further it is by standing on the shoulders of giants.'

SIR ISAAC NEWTON

Writing this book has only been possible because of the generosity of the hundreds of people we have worked with and interviewed over the past ten years, and most particularly over the past 18 months.

These extraordinary people have shared their time, their wisdom, their opinions and even criticisms and objections. All of this has helped this become a better book than it might have otherwise been.

To all of you, we say: Thank you. We are forever grateful.

A special thanks is also owed to a handful of people who went way above and beyond in helping us test our theories, ideas and thinking across different industries and countries, allowing us to pressure test the content of this book and ensure that it would resonate universally.

You have our deepest appreciation:

Dr Adam Fraser, human performance researcher, author, educator and consultant, Sydney, Australia

Adam Voigt, education expert, Melbourne, Australia

Alan Brodie, Alan Brodie Representation, London, England

Andrew Morello, Head of Business Development Yellow Brick Road, Sydney, Australia

Anouk Lagae, Duvel, Brussels, Belgium

Sir Antony Jay, writer, CVO, CBE, England

Bradley Trevor Greive, best-selling author of *The Blue Day Book*, Los Angeles, US

Brett King, Moven, New York, US

Bronnie Ware, author of *The Top Five Regrets of the Dying*, Sydney, Australia

Chip Bell, Customer Loyalty Authority, Greensboro, US

Chris Helder, international keynote speaker and author of best-selling books *Useful Belief, The Ultimate Book of Influence* and *Cut the Noise*, Melbourne, Australia

Cory Muscara international teacher and speaker on mindfulness, *Dr Oz* show regular, New York, US

Creel Price, Investable, Sydney, Australia

Dan Diamond, MD and resilience expert, Bremerton, US

David Bitton, Bitton, Sydney, Australia

Dermot Crowley, executive productivity expert and author of *Smart Work* and *Smart Teams*, Sydney, Australia

Frank Ribuot, CEO Randstad, Sydney, Australia

Holly Ransom, CEO Emergent and co-chair of UN Youth G20 Summit, Melbourne, Australia

Gabrielle Dolan, authority in business storytelling, founder at Jargon Free Fridays, author of *Stories for Work*, Melbourne, Australia

Gary Pittard, Pittard Training, Sydney, Australia

Captain Greg Laxton, Royal Australian Navy, Sydney, Australia

Irene Read, Director of Sales, BBC Worldwide

James Arvanitakis, Pro Vice-Chancellor (Research and Graduate Studies) WSU, Sydney, Australia

Jamie Pride, technologist, entrepreneur and author of *Unicorn Tears*, Sydney, Australia

Janine Garner, expert in networking, collaboration and leadership, author of *It's Who You Know*, Sydney, Australia

ACKNOWLEDGEMENTS

Jason Forrest, CEO FPG, Fort Worth, US

Dr Jason Fox, arch-wizard of The Cleverness, once 'Keynote Speaker of the Year', leadership and motivation design pioneer, Melbourne, Australia

Jonathan Lynn, Director, Producer, Writer, Actor, Bath, UK

Jeffrey Hayzlett, C-Suite Network, New York and South Dakota US

Karen and Roy Merricks, MTA, Queensland, Australia

Layne Beachley AO, world champion surfer, Sydney, Australia

Libby Trickett OAM, Olympic swimmer and gold medalist, Brisbane, Australia

Lisa Messenger, Founder & Editor in Chief, Collective Hub, Sydney, Australia

Lisa O'Neill, speaker, author, influencer, New Zealand.

Lisa Ronson, Tourism Australia, Sydney, Australia

Marion Farrelly, Absolutely Farrelly, Sydney, Australia

Mark Mathews, big wave surfer, Australia

Martin Mackay, Managing Director CA Technologies, Asia Pacific, Singapore

Marshall Goldsmith, Marshall Goldsmith Inc, Rancho Santa Fe, US

Matina Jewell, UN peacekeeper, Kingscliff, Australia

Matt Church, founder and chair of Thought Leaders and author of *Thought Leaders*, *Amplifiers*, *Next* and *Think*, Sydney, Australia

Michael Henderson, Cultures at Work, Auckland, New Zealand

Michael Smith, 2016 Australian Adventurer of the Year, proprietor of the Sun Theatre, Yarraville, Australia

Michelle Toft, Pink Lady® Apples, London, UK

Natalie Field, Australia Post, Melbourne, Australia

Neil Hereford, Global Head of Environmental Markets Commonwealth Bank, London, UK

Neil Plumridge, Managing Partner Consulting PwC, Melbourne, Australia

Nick Cowdery, ret. public prosecutor, former barrister and acting judge, Sydney, Australia

Oscar Trimboli, author of *Deep Listening* and *Breakthroughs*, Sydney, Australia

Peter Baines, Hands Across The Water, Sydney, Australia and Thailand

Peter Cook, CEO, Thought Leaders Business School, Melbourne, Australia

Peter Sheahan, founder and CEO Karrikins Group, Denver, US

Phillip Di Bella, Di Bella Coffee, Queenstown, New Zealand

Richard de Cresigny, Pilot and author of QF32 and Fly!

Richard Field, Viva Africa Group, Port Louis, Mauritius

Scott Bales, Innovation Labs, Singapore

Shep Hyken, Customer Service Expert at Hyken, St. Louis, US

Stephen Koukoulas, economist and former economic adviser to the Australian Prime Minister, Canberra, Australia

Tony Harris, Tony Harris BSU, Sydney, Australia

Trent Innes, Xero, Melbourne, Australia

We would also like to thank the many clients and their teams we have the privilege of working with, the speaker bureaus who make it possible to share our message with audiences all around the world, the Thought Leaders community, the BBC and of course to our audiences who give us their time, attention and laughter.

To Nicola Ruitenberg, our Business Manager, thanks for keeping us on track and in line.

To Ali Hiew thanks for editing this book with thought, cleverness and a sense of humour.

ACKNOWLEDGEMENTS

To Oli Sansom, photographer extraordinaire, for the Forever Skills cover photography.

To our team Wiley; Lucy Raymond, Chris Shorten, Ingrid Bond, Marie-Anna Sultani, Renee Aurish, Markus Taylor, Paul Ashley, Clare Dowdell thanks for bringing this book to market.

Finally to our families and friends thank you for forever being there for us: Thank you Gary, Darcy, Tony, Mike, Jodie & Bronwyn and Kerryanne, Lillah, Brian, Bruce & Simone.

forever : for a limitless time

skills : a learned power of doing something competently

: a developed aptitude or ability.

: the ability to use one's knowledge effectively and readily in execution or performance.

INTRODUCTION

Where might we find certainty in a world of change?

The Greek philosopher Heraclitus is famously quoted as observing that 'Change is the only constant in life'. We're not so sure.

Now, you're probably thinking, 'Wow, it's paragraph one and already they're questioning one of the key tenets of a renowned Greek philosopher. That's a bit bold!' And perhaps it is. But this book is all about challenging that theory (or, more precisely, the word 'only') and answering questions such as:

- Are some things evergreen?
- What do we want to hold on to?
- What, if anything, is forever?

Now don't get us wrong — clearly the point Heraclitus was making is still a very relevant reminder that change is inevitable and we should prepare ourselves accordingly. However, we also believe it's worth considering what other things will not fundamentally change, and how this understanding might actually prepare future generations, our organisations, and, indeed, ourselves, for whatever change awaits us in the future.

We're not alone. We've interviewed and surveyed hundreds of extraordinary people from around the world — leaders, practitioners and professionals from virtually every field of endeavour — in an effort to discover which skills they have most relied on to achieve their success and the skills they believe will always matter. (A more thorough explanation of our research methodology can be found in the three appendices at the end of this book.)

This journey has led us to the 12 skills that we believe will hold us in good stead, regardless of how the world changes.

We're not arguing with the fact that there is a lot of change happening all around us — merely that the true nature of that change is more complicated and nuanced than how it is typically presented to us.

And look, we get it; technology is evolving at a mind-blowing pace, information is spreading at the speed of 'likes', and even the physical environment around us is altering faster than ever before. None of this will surprise you. You might even be bored, or even numbed, by this observation, given how much attention has been focused on the rate of change in the media, in politics and in corporate culture.

In fact, it's become quite fashionable for futurists, economists and business strategists to terrify their audiences with dystopian views of the not-too-distant future characterised by Artificial Intelligence (AI) taking our jobs, algorithms hacking our most private moments and Austrian-accented cyborgs raising our children:

- 'Your job has been automated!'
- 'Your education is outdated!'
- 'Your workplace is under threat!'
- 'You're falling behind!'
- 'Those you care about are in imminent danger!'
- 'Come with me if you want to live!'

All of this fear drives clicks, shares, conversations, a whole lot of anxiety and, let's be honest, makes a lot of people a great deal of money.

So into this sea of panic and confusion, we'd like to launch a raft of calm. Throughout this book, we will identify skills-based lodestars by which we can navigate the choppy waters of change and develop capabilities that will endure and transcend the maelstrom of workplace trends and technological advances.

So yes, we do live in a constant state of flux, of technological change and disruption. A logical strategy for life and business is to accept the inevitability of change. However, we also believe that there are other constants worth considering: evergreen skills, character traits, values and roles that will be useful, powerful and differentiating regardless of what changes around us. Skills that can be learned, invested in and developed.

We call these 'Forever Skills'.

This isn't a book about survival or safety. We're not interested in minimum requirements. That would be far too ordinary, and there are already more than enough people in the world living lives of compromised impact and happiness.

No, we want you to do so much more than just 'get by'. And we wish for your children to choose out of possibility, not fear or scarcity.

We believe that your teams should be *lit up*, not just *putting up* with the change that they feel is being thrust upon them.

We want you to be the kind of leader who guides people through change to something better, not the kind who reacts blindly in panic.

You see, no matter what the future holds, we need people willing to *make positive change* and *make change positive*.

We will — forever.

The Three Spheres of Change

We typically think of change primarily in terms of what's changing. No great surprise, given our brains have evolved to view change as mostly threatening (often with good reason). So it stands to reason that we have a heightened sensitivity to the changes that occur in our environment, in technology and even in the moods of the people around us. We talk about it, hypothesise about it, evangelise it and complain about it. We try and predict it, manage it and keep up with it — and we often panic about it.

However, change has multiple dimensions and, consequently, multiple impacts. If we are to adequately prepare ourselves for an 'unpredictable future' we should take a more complete view of change. Our goal in this book is to broaden our emotional palette from one of fear and panic to one of calm acceptance and even inspiration.

Through our work and research in the worlds of professional training, business strategy leadership development and innovation consulting over the past decade, we have identified three critical areas of change. These three aspects inform how well people and businesses perform in an environment of change and also identify where their focus should be applied in terms of skills, strategy and investment in both time and resources.

We call these the Three Spheres of Change.

These Three Spheres of Change, while related, tend to drive significantly different outcomes, emotional responses and approaches. If used cleverly they give you a more complete view of change and how to manage it, drive it, lead it and not feel sick about it. Remember, one of our primary goals with this book is to remove much of the hype and panic around change so we can approach it with a more balanced perspective.

THE THREE SPHERES OF CHANGE™

The Three Spheres of Change are shown in figure 1.1:

1. what's changing

2. what's unchanging

3. what needs changing.

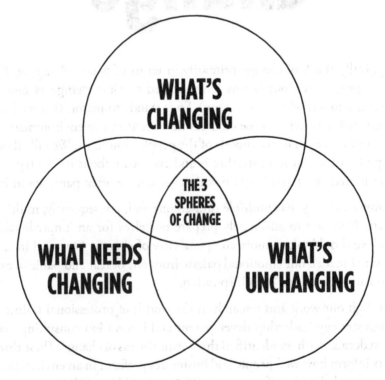

Figure 1.1 the Three Spheres of Change

The Three Spheres of Change are all important and should get equal attention. But they don't. Rather, some tend to get the preferential treatment and focus of a favoured child in a 1970s television sitcom.

What's changing is clearly the first and favourite child (the Marcia) and it gets the lion's share of our focus. It's bold, it's in your face and it commands attention now. It is the most reactionary sphere and when we filter our views through it, if we're not careful (and balanced by the other spheres), we can feel the need to take immediate action or else risk being left behind. This sphere drives business, technology, education and media who pump us up with worrying news about the importance of staying ahead. It is competitive.

What needs changing benefits from our bias towards the new and the excitement of fresh possibilities. It's wide-eyed and promise-filled. This might be considered 'the baby' (the Cindy) of the change family. Used well, this sphere is proactive. It can help you not simply react but create the changes you want to see in your business, community or world. Entrepreneurs tend to spend quite a bit of time here.

What's unchanging however, is the Jan Brady of change! It gets the least amount of attention when compared to the other two spheres, as it's quieter and less demanding. It's not as flashy as *What's changing* or as beguiling as *What needs changing*, but it is crucial if you want a full view of change. It brings much-needed perspective. It does this by taking a broader view of change. It's about human nature and our eternal needs and wants. It's perhaps the most important sphere when it comes to navigating change and preparing ourselves for the future.

This 'middle child' of change tends to overlay quite nicely the 'Not urgent but important' quadrant of Dr Stephen Covey's famous Urgent/Important Matrix, described in his self-help classic *The 7 Habits of Highly Successful People*. Like the 'Not urgent but important' quadrant, 'What's unchanging' doesn't seek immediate attention. However, an investment in it reduces fear and urgency and, in doing so, creates a sense of personal power and control.

Consequently, this is where we have focused most of our research and interviews for this book. There are already plenty of great books on the shelf about social trends and technological advances, and another significant proportion of recommended reading is devoted to innovation, new skills that will be required and how to make new change stick.

Forever Skills, however, aims to articulate what is worth keeping, nurturing and deepening.

So why is change such a big deal anyway?

FUTURE FEARS

Traditionally, human beings don't do change well. In fact, our social and commercial histories are peppered with examples of resistance to change, from the Luddites protesting the rise of weaving machines in the early 1800s to the famously failed 'New Coke' experiment that almost destroyed one of the most powerful brands and businesses on the planet.

Human beings, it seems, are quite backward when it comes to moving forward.

Today, that sense of alarm is exacerbated by the overwhelming stream of 'if it bleeds it leads'–style news reporting and 'alternative facts' flooding digital technology as never before. This can lead us to second-guess what we assume to be true and, in turn, drive us to be more paranoid and fearful than we once may have been.

We've conducted surveys around this fear of change with our audiences. While it does tend to increase as the average age of the audience rises, our surveys have demonstrated that the fear is actually quite universal. In fact, a simple shift in the frame we use to describe the nature of the change (for instance, looking at change in terms of housing affordability) can elicit a sense of dread even among digitally native Millennials and Gen Z's.

But this is far more than just a social trend or an existential crisis. In *The Art of Innovation*, Apple's former chief evangelist Guy Kawasaki notes that few market leaders have been able to 'jump the curve' and maintain leadership once a technological leap has been made.

Kawasaki observes that ice farmers in the frozen north failed to make the leap to factory-based ice production, who in turn failed to make the leap to the production and distribution of home refrigerators. This pattern has been replicated in many industries in the years since.

There are a number of reasons for this, not least of which is the fact that innovation requires a willingness and ability to kill the status quo. Not easy to do when you are actually part of the status quo and it also happens to pay your salary, cover your rent, take care of your children's school fees and put food on your table.

The other, perhaps more sinister, force increasing this sense of trepidation about the future is the fact that there is a lot of money and power to be earned from fear. Entire industries thrive on this very human emotion and have little interest in dispelling fear or creating a sense of comfort about the future.

These include sectors such as insurance, politics, education, religion, the stock market, banking and even retail. Areas that in many ways play a positive role in society, but are also susceptible to using fear-based manipulation.

So if fear is often an incorrect (or unhelpful) response to the world of change, what are the alternatives?

EMBRACING NEW OPPORTUNITIES

Perhaps just as distracting as future fear is the temptation offered by new opportunities.

At first blush, this seems a far less dangerous preoccupation than fear. Surely the capacity to find opportunity in change is a good thing. Of course, it can be. However, as anyone who has ever sported a mullet or worn yoga pants for anything other than a yoga class can (and should) attest, not every trend or opportunity is worth investing in.

In much the same way that we can become distracted by what's changing, we can also become enamoured with what could, or we believe *should*, change.

This is partly driven by the competitive desire, which many of us share, to be the first and to shape the future in our own image.

However, as Ohio State University's Oded Shenkar suggests in his book *Copycats: How smart companies use imitation to gain a strategic edge*, being first to market is not always a recipe for success. In fact, Shenkar's research found that as much as 97.8 per cent of the value of an innovation goes to the imitators, not the innovators. So much for being first to market!

Which is not to say that a mindset of openness to change or an awareness of opportunity is always a liability. Quite the contrary. However, in the same way that the trends, tools and technologies that are changing are not the complete picture of change, neither is the change we seek to make ourselves.

So, rather than stifling innovation and curtailing progressive strategy, what we're advocating for is a more holistic view of change where just as much focus is paid to what remains as to what we might lose or gain.

RE-THINKING EDUCATION AND TRAINING

All of this becomes particularly important when viewed through the lens of education.

This is true whether it's applied to our own personal development, the training protocols we implement with our teams, or our children's educations.

Of all the industries we've had the pleasure of working with throughout our professional careers, few incite such passionate opinion and disagreement as education. Which is not entirely surprising, as we're all the products of that industry, and it was a process that was not necessarily enjoyed by all.

This anxiety has seen a rise in trends such as helicopter parenting, increasing demands on the content of curriculums, and parents becoming more emphatic and opinionated in parent–teacher interviews.

The media regularly reports and endorses cries from parents pressing for a 'return to basics', to 'teach the three Rs' and the 'need for more STEM' (or its more recent modification, 'STEAM' — Science, Technology, Engineering, Art and Mathematics).

Of course, much of this is reactionary and subject to the same trends and fashions that drive change in the worlds of business, society and government.

One of the critical reasons we wrote this book, having invested a significant portion of our lives into training leaders and teams in different industries around the world, is because playing catch-up, or trying to predict which skill will fall into or out of favour, has proven to be a largely flawed strategy.

One of the great challenges of change is that it is unpredictable. There's a reason futurists, social demographers and economists don't offer money-back guarantees.

Having observed the limits and challenges of modern education, what came through repeatedly in our research was the idea that a new conception of education, one based on self-learning, was critical for any skills we might need in the future, and that the process of education is a lifetime undertaking.

Nonetheless, as we'll explain in the coming chapters, our research also revealed that there is a set of skills, traits and capabilities — Forever Skills — that can help all of us adapt and prosper through change, while equipping us with a framework for whatever new skills might be required.

THE THREE KEY AREAS OF FOREVER SKILLS

In the interest of clarity, memorability and portability, we began to cluster the Forever Skills around three central themes.

Clustering skills, and indeed choosing the correct names for these skills, presented us with a few issues. Throughout our research we learned that what we had assumed were easily understood descriptors for certain skills varied greatly across different industries and contexts. We also wanted to create a mnemonic that was memorable and usable, but not so trivial that it devalued the thinking and collective wisdom that sat behind it.

We decided on three key groups. The first revolves around an ability to understand, strategise for and solve complicated problems. The language that emerged around this cluster includes a capacity to solve problems with different modes of thinking: creativity, critical thinking, insight mapping, design, strategy and situational intelligence.

The second cluster that emerged centres around people skills. This includes the ability to persuade, to move others to action and engage and galvanise support for one's ideas.

Lastly, the third cluster centres on the idea of control. This includes controlling our own performance under duress, our own fear, the quality of our output, the environment (in its broadest definition) and others — in terms of consensus building, social justice and crime prevention.

All three of these clusters reveal themselves throughout our skills research, throughout the history of work and human endeavour, in our present workplaces and also in the predictions of futurists and economists about the near and distant future. Which makes them forever.

So what are the three Forever Skills clusters?

1. *Creativity.* The capacity to garner insights, invent, innovate, solve problems and be mentally agile.

2. *Communication.* The ability to engage, persuade and move others towards a shared goal.

3. *Control.* The mastery of power over self, our actions, the environment and social consensus.

Within each of these three clusters sit four crucial skills. Now to explore these 12 skills that will be evergreen.

PART 1

CREATIVITY
SKILLS

'THE BEST WAY TO PREDICT THE FUTURE IS TO CREATE IT.'

Peter Drucker (or possibly Abraham Lincoln or maybe Alan Kaye)

The first of our Forever Skills clusters is *Creativity*.

Unfortunately, even though we've identified this as a critical cluster of Forever Skills, most people don't actually believe they are creative.

It's likely you're one of them. Research done by Adobe in 2012 found that eight in ten people felt that unlocking creativity is critical to economic growth, and almost two thirds believed creativity is valuable to society. Yet, only a paltry one in four believed they are living up to their own creative potential.

Adobe's research correlates with our own experience. We regularly ask conference attendees and boardrooms filled with people to raise their hands if they think of themselves as creative. Usually, out of the tens, hundreds or even thousands of audience members, only a few will put up their hands.

In a world where robots are predicted to dominate the replicable processes in our work, leaving the more creative tasks to us humans, this is not a good result.

Creative skills are particularly important because they help us solve problems, find new ways to do things, challenge the status quo and ultimately move the human race forward. Creativity, therefore, is a key area of Forever Skills and it's one we all need to develop.

The question is, Why don't we think we're creative?

Perhaps it's because we seem to think creativity is something that happens magically or intrinsically, as opposed to something we make happen. Consider some of the language we use around new ideas and creativity. It was 'an act of genius', 'a flash of inspiration', a moment when 'the muse struck', or that 'the idea just came to me'. All of these clichés reinforce the misguided notion that creativity is a mysterious force available only to the special few, or something that happens randomly or as a result of luck.

While a solution may indeed occur to us seemingly out of nowhere, the reality is that we have probably been working on the problem, even subconsciously, for some time—gathering stimulus and input and attempting to solve it.

Compounding the perception of creativity as random and fickle is the fact that many people are confused about what creativity actually is. At a conference recently, we were lucky enough to sit on a panel discussing the importance of creativity in business. One of the other panelists was a very intelligent, highly educated senior leader from an enormous global technology company. She enthusiastically regaled the audience with her tale of how the company's staff now occupied some of their time with painting, drawing and even sculpting to demonstrate their commitment to creativity.

Sigh.

Let's dispel some myths about creativity.

Creativity is not artistry. It's not an ability to draw, or play music, or even to imagine a compelling fictional story. In fact, these tasks can sometimes (although not always) be rather formulaic exercises in replication.

Computers have in fact already composed songs, written advertisement copy and are more than capable of creating, in either intricate detail or loose inky lines, portraits and landscapes in the style of any great artist you can name. Software applications even offer filters that you can apply to make 'art' happen in an instant.

Rather, creativity is an ability to think, to solve problems in ways we haven't seen before. It is innovation, flexibility, agility, ingenuity and mental fluidity. All things that will be incredibly useful for our ongoing success, no matter what the future brings.

In our experience, creativity is more discipline than talent. It is something we can practise and improve on, which makes it very much a skill, and a vital one at that.

As we move into the workplaces and roles of the future, in an age of disruption, we will need to be able to apply 'creativity on demand', to solve problems that seem to have no precedent or replicable solutions.

There is much debate about how quickly artificial intelligence will be in our future workplaces, and how dominant it will be, however, what is abundantly clear is that AI will substantially affect work as we know it. AI is already extremely good at anything that requires repetition and crunching large volumes of data, which leads us to believe 'If we can replicate it, we will automate it'.

This means that as the world increases its use of AI, creative skills will become even more critical.

Of course, creativity has always been important. Einstein, in explaining his methods of exploration, said he imagined riding on the end of a light beam. Marie Curie was famously curious about how the world worked. Edison said he had not failed to create the light bulb but rather had discovered over 10 000 ways not to, and Walt Disney famously remarked, 'It's kind of fun to do the impossible.'

We're also quite sure that our prehistoric ancestors, those who for the first time fashioned tools, harnessed fire and invented the wheel, would also have spoken highly of the power of invention and the ability to see things in new and different ways — we just don't have quote libraries that go back that far.

Creativity drives progress. It advances and enhances us. This rather strongly suggests we will always need it.

So which creative skills will be forever?

Through our research we've identified four creativity skills that promise to be in high demand, not just in spite of change, but because of it:

1. insight

2. conversion

3. problem solving

4. agility.

Let's examine these creative Forever Skills more closely.

Insight

The ability to identify opportunities and make intelligent judgements has been, and always will be, critical.

To thrive in the future, possessing information alone will not be enough. In fact, access to information does not necessarily lead to success, nor to accuracy in predicting the future. Rather, success lies in the ability to transform information into insight through creativity and judgement. In other words, *thinking* is still going to be an important function, no matter how much data we gather.

Consider the majority of forecasts that pollsters were making just prior to the 2016 US presidential election. You may recall that most predicted Donald Trump was not only unlikely to win, he was even described as a 'sideshow distraction' that wouldn't come close. Even on election day, some pundits gave him just a 15 per cent chance of winning. Obviously, they were quite wrong, despite having access to some of the most advanced information-gathering technology in history.

Exactly the same thing happened in the UK's Brexit vote. Despite copious quantities of computer-gathered data, forecasters failed to predict the eventual outcome.

People were shocked. How could these major events be so wrongly forecast, given the times in which we live?

THE LURE OF DATA

It seems that even in an era where we create 2.5 quintillion bytes of data every day, where computers can skim data sets and judge the mood of a workplace or even a country, human behaviour remains a little unpredictable (with all due respect to Dan Ariely's excellent 2008 book, *Predictably Irrational*).

Data is powerful (and we are big fans of getting as much of it as we can), but without insight, meaning-making and creativity applied to this raw information, it might be compared to a tree falling in a forest with no-one around. Does it make a sound?

In other words, data requires meaning to become more than mere numbers.

CRITICAL FACTORS MAKING INSIGHT A FOREVER SKILL:

- **Data requires sense-making to give it meaning.**
- **Data is only as reliable as its quality, completeness and focus.**
- **Good judgement must sometimes be exercised in imperfect conditions.**

No matter how much information we have accumulated, or how clever our data is, we will always need to overlay human insight and interpretation across it. Human beings are still needed to *make* sense of it and *create* meaning. The verbs used in this last sentence are particularly important.

This means we need people who can breathe life into the numbers and generate numerous outcomes and scenarios from them. With insight we can develop multiple ways of reaching our objectives and make richer decisions in increasingly complicated circumstances.

In fact, it is those who can generate insight, and imagine impacts and consequences well beyond the accumulated knowledge and precedent they have access to, who have succeeded throughout history and will continue to do so in the future.

It wasn't candle makers who imagined light globes, nor telegraph operators who dreamed up the telephone. Not only did taxi drivers not conceive of Uber, they have done much to undermine it in an attempt to preserve the status quo.

Truthfully, the data on all of these existing business models was probably quite reassuring just before they were disrupted; sales were probably decent (perhaps even good), and the business models may have seemed rather robust. However, numbers rarely point to how an entire category might be reimagined.

In this context, it's useful to think of insight as a 'judgement about the meaning of facts', to pinch a turn of phrase from Richard P Rumelt's *Good Strategy/Bad Strategy*.

What we must also remember about data is that it is largely a game of probabilities and likelihoods. The thing is, odds are not absolutes or certainties. If something has an 80 per cent chance of occurring, there is still a 20 per cent chance that it will not. And of course, that's a simple two-outcome example. In real life, outcomes are rarely binary. Life is neither linear nor tidy.

Having said that, this is one of the primary reasons we like to lean on data so heavily. It tends to clean life up for us.

Think about the standard deviation graph, or 'bell curve', as it's more commonly known, as a visualisation of this data-driven tidiness. Before we 'smooth out' the data for reasons of interpretive assessment or like-for-like comparisons, there is considerably more natural variance. People or behaviours that vary wildly at either end of the data set are often neatly pruned off and smaller variations are massaged into a pleasing curve.

Of course, this can be extremely useful, but it's worth remembering that this is a sanitised picture of reality with extremes and outliers often taken out of consideration. And let's not forget: sometimes it is these extremes that change the world for the better.

This means we will always need to combine data and information with judgement, observation, interpretation, logic and experience, suspicions, guesses and even gut responses to make sense and create meaning. In doing so, the data can be used to generate new ideas. To create change. To make progress. To imagine what doesn't yet exist.

Great minds have always known this and, in order to thrive forever, we must all do the same.

In order to increase our insight skills, we should consider adding the following tools and techniques to our repertoire:

1. Learn to read the signs and look for patterns.

2. Be aware of biases.

3. Sit on the other side of the argument.

4. Seek to understand (not just analyse).

5. Make meaning from the information you have gathered.

1 LEARN TO READ THE SIGNS AND LOOK FOR PATTERNS

Clearly we're not talking about reading tea leaves (although human curiosity about the future may make fortune-telling a Forever Skill too, regardless of scepticism from some quarters).

In this instance, however, what we are talking about is the capacity to recognise the signposts that are available to all of us if we would just pay enough attention.

Digital futurist and founder of Innovation Labs Singapore Scott Bales considers insight one of the key skills he uses in his business and work. He told us that three things drive insight:

i. Learning to recognise patterns.

ii. Connecting the dots or looking for what links that which seems to be disconnected.

iii. Seeking to cross-pollinate from one area to another (more on this later when we talk about the skill of conversion in chapter 3).

All of these are ways in which we can improve our ability to read the cues and clues that are all around us, to be more observant and catch the connections that will assist us in developing greater understanding.

'Ideas rose in crowds; I felt them collide until pairs interlocked, so to speak, making a stable combination.' These are the wise words of Henri Poincaré, a French polymath who talked about creativity's role in science in his 1955 tome, *The Foundations of Science*. Poincaré understood that connecting ideas by recognising patterns was at the core of the work of a scientist.

Of course, this line of thinking does not only apply to scientists. Great investors also know how to 'read between the columns', Stephen Koukoulas, an economist who has guided global banking corporations as well as prime ministers, told us. 'You have to be able to read more than the numbers. Everyone has access to the same stuff. What matters is the way you reach your conclusions.'

Koukoulas went on to tell us the story of an economist who had developed their own unique economic test, 'The Oxford Street test'. (Oxford Street is a fashionable shopping strip in a well-off suburb of inner Sydney.) 'While most economists used to rely mostly on analysing charts and graphs, this economist simply walked down Oxford Street and looked at how many *For Lease* signs they saw.'

The signs that this economist was reading went well beyond numbers. The economist was taking the economy's temperature using things such as people's moods, their shopping habits, business successes and the areas in which they could be seen.

Likewise, the 'Lipstick Effect' has long been spoken about in marketing and economic circles. This theory is the result of people reading the signs (when economic times are tough lipstick sales go up and big-ticket-item sales go down). Experience and an understanding of people, sales and the climate in which he traded led Leonard Lauder of Estée Lauder to make the connection.

Clair Jennifer, founder of Australian fashion brand Wombat, chooses locations for new stores based on 'leafy trees and fluffy dogs'. These things are a cultural yardstick by which she measures her stores' likelihood of success. Now, 'fluffy dogs and leafy streets' may sound about as far from scientific enquiry as you can get, but in fact it is a very distilled way of thinking. What Clair is actually doing is reading and tracking the psychographics of her customers in a way that purely demographic information or statistical population studies might miss.

However, signs and signals are not always so obvious. We need to develop our observational skills and push beyond our own expectations and beliefs. Like most skills, insight is learned and earned.

Johann Wolfgang von Goethe observed that *'Man sieht was man weiss'*, which roughly translates to 'You see what you know'.

Which is a prescient reminder that a large part of being creative and generating useful insight is an awareness of our own predilections and working hard to compensate for them, or at least not let them blind us to alternative possibilities.

2 BE AWARE OF BIASES

There is a wonderful scene in the classic BBC situation comedy *Yes Prime Minister* written by the very talented Antony Jay and Jonathan Lynn, in which two of the core characters, public service bureaucrats Sir Humphrey Appleby and Bernard, are speaking about a problematic opinion poll.

HUMPHREY: *Well, have another opinion poll done showing the voters are AGAINST bringing back national service.*

BERNARD: *They can't be for it AND against it.*

HUMPHREY: *Oh, of course they can, Bernard …*

(Demonstrating the required methodology)

Mr Woolley, are you worried about the number of young people without jobs?

BERNARD: *Yes.*

HUMPHREY: *Are you worried about the rise in crime among teenagers?*

BERNARD: *Yes.*

HUMPHREY: *Do you think there's a lack of discipline in our comprehensive schools?*

BERNARD: *Yes.*

HUMPHREY: *Do you think young people welcome some authority and leadership in their lives?*

BERNARD: *Yes.*

HUMPHREY: *Do you think they respond to a challenge?*

BERNARD: *Yes.*

HUMPHREY: *Would you be in favour of reintroducing national service?*

BERNARD: *Oh. Well, I suppose I might be.*

HUMPHREY: *Yes or no?*

BERNARD: *Yes.*

HUMPHREY: *Of course you would, Bernard. After all you've told me, you can't say no to that. So, they don't mention the first five questions and they publish the last one.*

BERNARD: *Is that really what they do?*

HUMPHREY: *Not the reputable ones, no ... but there aren't many of those. Alternatively, you can get the opposite result.*

BERNARD: *How?*

HUMPHREY: *Mr Woolley, are you worried about the danger of war?*

BERNARD: *Yes.*

HUMPHREY: *Are you worried about the growth of armaments?*

BERNARD: *Yes.*

HUMPHREY: *Do you think there's a danger in giving young people guns and teaching them how to kill?*

BERNARD:	*Yes.*
HUMPHREY:	*Do you think it's wrong to force people to take up arms against their will?*
BERNARD:	*Yes.*
HUMPHREY:	*Would you oppose the reintroduction of national service?*
BERNARD:	*Yes.*
HUMPHREY:	*There you are, you see, Bernard. The perfect balanced sample. So we just commission our own survey for the Ministry of Defence. See to it, Bernard.*

Like all great humour there is an incisive truth here. The writers of the show clearly understood that research is almost always incomplete, intrinsically flawed and rarely neutral.

Now, this is not to say we shouldn't use research — far from it. In fact, we have relied pretty heavily on research (discussed in the appendices) generated by ourselves and others in preparing for and writing this book.

Rather, we're simply taking Goethe's advice and being conscious of our bias towards our own filters, values and experience.

3 SIT ON THE OTHER SIDE OF THE ARGUMENT

One of the problems with traditional innovation workshops, or hackathons, is that many times we have the wrong people sitting around the table. Often we are asking the very people who benefit from the status quo to break that system and redesign something else. Unconsciously we are asking them to undermine their own sense of competence, survival and safety.

All human beings, to a greater or lesser degree, are influenced by loss aversion. This means we are generally more afraid of losing what we have than we are excited by the prospect of gaining something better. ('Better the devil you know.') This fear of losing can be a trap. It stops us stretching, keeps us where we are and can rob us of opportunity.

This is one of the reasons we retitled our innovation workshops as 'Risk Prototyping'. This, it turns out, is much easier for organisations to buy and a lot less risky for team members to engage with.

Essentially, we get organisations and teams to imagine what might threaten their business model or replace them in the marketplace. The stated goal is to 'Prepare for and mitigate risk'. What we're actually doing is training them to design and create the very thing they are afraid could happen so that they might be forewarned and develop a strategy accordingly.

The reasoning is quite simple: 'What could our competitors do that would make us very worried?' We then advise the leadership team to explore that possibility before their competition does.

Screenwriters in Hollywood were used in a similar way post 9/11 to help US Homeland Security 'prototype' scenarios for further terrorist attacks. This allowed military strategists to plan for possible outcomes, proving imagination can be a critical asset even in the very serious world of national security.

In reality, our Risk Prototyping process is almost identical to an innovation workshop we might run, but, crucially, the frame of reference is different. We're asking people to create from a position of protecting what they know, as opposed to upending their own world.

This allows the team to be more open, more willing to experiment and able to truly imagine what could be disruptive for their business.

This kind of contrary thinking is an extremely useful tool in gaining insight and generating creativity.

Professor Sidney Dekker is an expert in the very sensible world of Workplace Safety, although, unlike many of his peers, he tends to have quite contrarian views.

Sidney told us, 'Too much safety thinking is oriented from the perspective of what is wrong, and not enough looks at what is going right.' He himself has done studies in hospitals where the tendency is to look at behaviours that were present in times of error as opposed to behaviours at times when positive outcomes were achieved.

He found there was *no difference*. The behaviours were essentially the same. In other words, the different outcomes were not process-based but included others things, such as attitude, communication, a willingness to speak up and the ability to call 'stop' when things did not seem right.

Often times, insight is more about changing the question, being willing to explore a different hypothesis or diagnosis, than it is about generating more information. Borrowing some more wisdom from Rumelt's *Good Strategy/Bad Strategy,* 'In business, most deep strategic changes are brought about by a change in diagnosis — a change in the definition of a company's situation.'

4 SEEK TO UNDERSTAND (NOT JUST ANALYSE)

In his 1946 book *Psychology for Musicians,* Percy C Buck writes, 'An amateur can be satisfied with knowing a fact. A professional must know the reason why.'

We need to be as obsessed with *why* circumstances are as they are as we are with *what* is happening. In other words, rather than simply treating symptoms, we need to identify and correct the causes of dysfunction and error.

To do this we need to get among it.

Genchi Genbutsu is a Japanese phrase that means 'Go and see for yourself', or, roughly, 'Get your boots on'. It is an integral component of the Toyota Way.

Factory visits were a crucial part of the creative process we engaged in when we worked as creative and strategic directors early in our careers in advertising. We strove to interrogate the product, to see how it was made, bought and used. Going to the factory often allowed us to see things, to create distinctions and identify insights that most people had taken for granted or else missed completely.

Legendary Madison Avenue 'hot shop' Doyle Dane Bernbach used this method to generate advertisement headlines such as: 'Ever wonder how the man who drives the snowplow ... drives to the snowplow?', allowing Volkswagen to demonstrate its reliability in cold and extreme weather conditions.

David Ogilvy, another legend of the *Mad Men* era, used the same process to sell Rolls-Royces when, after driving one for himself, he discovered that 'At 60 miles an hour the loudest noise in the new Rolls-Royce comes from the electric clock.'

This experiential gathering of insight has applications far beyond the hedonistic offices of Madison Avenue.

Dr Natassia Goode is a senior research fellow in the Centre for Human Factors and Sociotechnical Systems at the University of the Sunshine Coast. She is an expert in system thinking and accident causation.

Natassia encourages businesses to use systems thinking models to analyse incidents in the workplace, rather than focussing on the behaviour of injured workers. She tells the story of the head of a freight transport company coming to her in exasperation with the company's high incidence of minor sprains and injuries. 'The managers had pretty much determined the cause of the problem; they didn't want me to start the analysis again. They had decided the problem was that the workers were just rushing.' she told us.

But Natassia had to see for herself. The company she was working with had located its head office and management far away from the airport and the tarmac where the actual freight handling took place. 'I always spend as much time observing as I can.'

Natassia talked to as many people in the chain as she could. She watched the workers themselves. In doing so she noticed that, despite items being clearly marked as two-person lifts, they were being lifted by only one. So she asked them about it and found out 'there just isn't enough staff...if we want to make the strict airline deadlines set in place we just have to get on with it and lift alone'.

When she asked management about this alleged lack of staff they told her the staffing numbers had not changed at all. She then asked the supervisors and discovered that, while the total staffing numbers had not changed, the number of permanent staff had. This meant far less of the staff could access all the areas of the tarmac and storage sheds (as only permanent staff were permitted due to access restrictions). The casual workforce needed supervision, which placed further pressure on the permanent staff.

'It wasn't one factor causing the injuries. It was not a lack of staff, but a lack of permanent staff combined with a system that people believed was rigid and airport imposed when, in truth, it wasn't at all..' No bad thing, but the knock-on effect was rather more complicated than 'Our people aren't doing what they're supposed to'!

'The solution was not singular. It required more staff with appropriate access, coupled with addressing the scheduling pressures and communication issues.'

This is understanding in action and you can see why it matters. Data alone could not solve the problem the freight handlers faced. The data was too raw, too singular. Natassia created a solution with multiple inputs. She went and understood for herself.

As she explains it, when we apply systems thinking to a problem we realise that solutions are rarely singular and often it is an unforeseen change that causes a system to break (making it hard to prepare for).

You need to get up close and personal with the problems you are solving. Clever people understand this. Creative people understand this.

5 MAKE MEANING FROM THE INFORMATION YOU HAVE GATHERED

Could data-driven AI have predicted that Steve Jobs and Steve Wozniak would have successfully competed with companies like IBM in the 1970s? This is what Richard Branson considers in an article written for Virgin.com in 2018. Clearly, Branson sees the value in interpreting meaning beyond simply what the numbers or status quo would lead us to believe.

Then, drawing the comparison between that observation and his own Virgin companies, he continues,

> *Traditional airline metrics were essentially screaming, 'This is crazy! It cannot work! Don't do it!' This is precisely why we didn't let data get in the way.*

In other words, the meaning you create trumps raw numbers. Sure, look at the numbers and be well informed, but also take time to look beyond the pure numbers and consider what *could* be, what *should* be, and even what *needs to be.*

'I'm especially concerned that people who are developing AI are doing so at the expense of developing human talent,' Branson explains, 'downgrading all the instincts and experiential learning that has propelled us from cave dwellings to today's modern societies.'

In other words, data is not an answer, it's input.

Our ability to make sense of things will always matter. A capacity to bring context, experience, relative (*and* unrelated) comparisons and intuition to the table. What robots and AI will struggle with is questions such as 'So what?' and 'What if?'

Meaning-making is not easy. It takes a lot of attention, wondering, exploring possibilities and bringing together various inputs to draw conclusions, develop good judgement and make powerful decisions. It sounds simple, but so do many things in retrospect.

This is one of the problems of referencing case studies in business and sharing stories in books. It always seems so linear, obvious and easy when you look at circumstances from the relative comfort of the story's end.

Confusion and missteps are omitted from the story for the sake of brevity, and uncertainty seems quite inconsequential when reduced to a paragraph or two in a white paper. The meaning appears to be reached so easily that we underestimate the effort that creating that meaning actually required.

Consider the case of carry-on spinners (suitcases with wheels, for the uninitiated). It seems like a no-brainer, yet we had landed on the moon before we thought to put wheels on suitcases.

In 1970 Bernard D Sadow was lugging two heavy suitcases through an airport when he saw a heavy piece of machinery being moved easily though the airport on a skid. He said to his wife, 'We should put wheels on suitcases.' (It was a perfect collision of problem and external input).

He dragged his heavy bags home and created a prototype. It worked, of course, although the uptake of the idea was slower than you'd expect. In fact, it took another 17 years for the carry-on suitcase as we know it today, with a telescopic handle and wheels on its base, to be invented and commercialised in the marketplace.

Incidentally, this commercialisation was initiated by a pilot who had obviously reached a breaking point, having inefficiently dragged suitcases around for years. Clearly, they too were in possession of some 'experiential insight'.

Today we cannot imagine heavy luggage with no wheels on it, and many might assume that we could have easily solved the problem ourselves. But the reality is it took more than just noticing how heavy bags were to carry — it required insight to recognise this as an opportunity.

Our minds are data banks filled with useful intelligence, but it requires insight to transform this 'inside information' into a new discovery.

A good friend of ours, Peter Cook, is the CEO of Thought Leaders. It's an organisation that helps smart people become commercially smart also.

He tells the story of going skiing with his wife, Trish. Now, both Peter and Trish are accomplished skiers, but Pete assures us, 'Trish is *way* better.'

On a ski holiday they enrolled in a high-performance ski school - essentially the training that ski instructors do.

As part of the preparation they both had to rate themselves out in a bunch of different categories (skiing bumps, jumping, steep slopes, etc.).

When Pete submitted their self-assessments to their guide he also somewhat sheepishly admitted that he had scored higher than Trish, even though she was definitely the stronger skier.

Don't worry, the instructor said, we always downgrade the assessment for men and upgrade it for women.

Now, aside from the sad state of affairs with regard to gender expectations and relative self-belief, this story also demonstrates the power of insight. The ski guide clearly had enough experience and insight to not simply trust the data given to them and had devised their own system, however rough and ready, to make the performance and results more reliable, and a lot less dangerous.

This is meaning-making in action. It's not simply trusting the numbers, but adding the numbers to our understanding, experience and instincts.

∞

Ultimately, data is incredibly valuable, but it is rarely a complete picture of reality. Creating meaning beyond numbers; countering our natural biases; using judgement and experience beyond statistics; and going and seeing for ourselves and using data as an input, not an answer, is crucial. Developing a capacity to transform raw data into meaning and value is a skill we will always need.

APPLICATION

FIVE STEPS FOR IMPROVING YOUR INSIGHT

1. Learn to read the signs and look for patterns.
2. Be aware of biases.
3. Sit on the other side of the argument.
4. Seek to understand (not just analyse).
5. Make meaning from the information you have gathered.

Conversion

We have always engaged with the skills of conversion: turning seeds into bread, coal into power and ideas into innovation.

Many years ago, before the names Harry, Hermione and Ron were anything more than the kind of names you might hear being called on a rather unremarkable prep-school register in the UK, human beings were sharing secret rumours, carrying out clandestine experiments and searching ancient texts — all in the pursuit of the Philosopher's Stone.

Of course, the Philosopher's Stone was no less a work of fiction than the Harry Potter novel of the same name, but its effects on the real world have been felt for generations.

Mentions of the Philosopher's Stone and alchemy go back hundreds and perhaps even thousands of years to ancient Greece, China, India and Egypt. The imaginations of alchemists, proto-scientists and fortune hunters have long been captivated by tales of this red, powdery substance that was believed to transmute base metals into *gold*!

In fact, this pursuit, whether driven by greed or the quest for knowledge, helped spark the scientific revolution that would ultimately relegate the story of alchemy and the Philosopher's Stone to the fairytale section of the bookstore and elevate science to the position of respect that it enjoys today (at least in some parts of the world).

What was so captivating about the story of alchemy, aside from the promise of being able to produce gold on demand, was the concept of conversion: being able to take something from one sphere of life and transfer it to another and, in doing so, increase its value and enrich our lives.

But conversion is far from a skill lost to the sands of time. In fact, this quest for transmutation, adaptation, re-framing, re-invention and re-interpretation is as relevant today as it has ever been.

Our capacity to convert raw materials (and even thoughts) into commercial assets or social institutions still defines success today. And in a world where the human appetite for consumption has left our supply of natural resources somewhat stretched, those skilled at conversion will be forever needed.

Rory Sutherland, in one of his infamous TED talks, inferred that 'intangible value', our capacity to convert ideas and thoughts into commercially valuable assets, was the ultimate act of environmentalism. If the only conversion happens entirely between the ears of the creator and those of the people they serve, no resources need to be dug up, harvested or chopped down.

CRITICAL FACTORS MAKING CONVERSION A FOREVER SKILL:

- **Products, services and tools tend to change but the emotional and psychological needs they satisfy often remain.**
- **Innovation and shifts in business models are many times the result of looking outside of an industry or category for inspiration.**
- **Recycling and up-cycling has always been with us and it's of increasing importance from an environmental and sustainability point of view.**

However, even though conversion is a skill almost as old as humanity itself, in an age where technology has rendered us almost immune to wonder, we're quite likely to ignore its increasing importance and become distracted by the new rather than the opportunity lying dormant in the used.

We can best develop these skills of conversion by doing the following:

1. Look for the big themes.
2. Transfer, mix and macro.
3. Be broadly interested and prodigiously curious.
4. Generate unexpected collisions.
5. Learn to repurpose like a child.

1 LOOK FOR THE BIG THEMES

When you become attuned to the universals in any task, no matter how humble, you never waste your time again. The simple act of 'stacking shelves may teach you about efficiency,' economist Stephen Koukoulas advises.

Successful people are constantly looking for lessons they can take and use elsewhere. In a way they're the ultimate recyclers: no experience goes to waste. Their mindset is one of, 'What can I take from this?'

Of course, this book is all about the 'big theme' of skills, a topic that itself also requires a capacity for conversion.

Depending on which economist or futurist you choose to speak to, the number of jobs, careers and employers the generation currently entering the workforce will have in their lifetime varies wildly. Add to that the rise of entrepreneurship and the 'gig economy' and you can probably round those numbers up without missing the mark by too great a margin.

Regardless of the accuracy or otherwise of these estimates, what is clear is that the workplace of the future will not be the workplace we currently know. We will likely work across many projects and take up various roles and responsibilities rather than having a single 'job' over the course of a number of years.

This means that it's critical to be able to take key concepts, experiences and skills and then redeploy them in new situations, applications and roles.

Being able to ladder up and identify the larger theme or context of a problem is often the first step to solving it — particularly when others are lost in the minutia of it.

A great example of this is the collaboration between London's Great Ormond Street Hospital and Ferrari.

In the 1990s, the hospital was experiencing issues transferring patients between departments, such as from the operating theatre back to the Intensive Care Unit.

Now, this is a hospital with an international reputation for high standards of care and for the professionalism of their people. Yet, despite the quality of their doctors, nurses and administrative staff, they were unable to bring the error rate down to what they considered an acceptable margin.

However, rather than getting lost in the granular detail of the process, they realised that the big thematic problem they were facing wasn't about surgery or even medical care in particular. It was all about *fast, accurate and critical transitions*.

So they did what most medical professionals do when they can't solve a problem: they called in a specialist. In this instance, a Ferrari Formula 1 racing pit crew.

The pit crew's transition was seen as analogous to the handoff between medical staff and, critically, they identified a role that was missing in their own handover: the role of the 'lollipop man' who waves the car in and coordinates the pit stop. This role was then assigned to the anaesthesiologist.

The result? Before the new handover protocol, patient equipment and information errors sat at approximately 30 per cent. Afterward, only 10 per cent occurred in both areas.

What we can learn from this collaboration is that correctly identifying the *kind* of problem (or problems) you need to solve is critical. It might be an efficiency problem, or a communication error or even a timing challenge. The point is, redefining the problem significantly affects the strategy and solutions that might be generated.

If you can see the pattern and understand the broad theme you need to apply your creativity to, you also create a sense of clarity about where to look for influences and ideas and solutions.

2 TRANSFER, MIX AND MACRO

In a more fluid workplace, hard skills won't necessarily transfer very easily — but many other skills will.

For example, a friend of ours worked for years as a lawyer before moving into the world of advertising. Now, many people were surprised at this seemingly unrelated career shift, but if you look for the commonalities between the two professions, you can see that the step is neither all that large nor terribly surprising.

Both use facts, emotion and persuasion to make a case, and both have to generate buy-in and work with clients to get them to the outcome they want. The similarities are there to be seen, but only once we have developed a skill for finding the universal in the specific and applying tools such as transference, mixing and macro-ing.

Declan Coffey is part of the senior leadership team of the technology company DXC Technology, despite the fact that he had never planned to work in IT.

Before taking up his leadership role with the technology giant, he was part of British retail department store John Lewis, but relinquished this role to pursue a life in art. In fact, his introduction to the world of technology was quite accidental. He literally bumped into an IT leader at a pub, got offered a job over a beer, and went on to have a stellar IT career. In his own words,

> *I was asking the guy from the IT company I'd just met about his business and trying to connect his challenges to things I had learned in retail. I was telling him my ideas and he said, 'Come and work for me.' I knew nothing about IT and they didn't know what to do with me for a while. But it all worked out.*

Coffey was able to transfer skills from one industry to another because he possessed the skills to identify what was industry transferrable.

Critical in the exercise of transference are the tools and techniques of 'mixing and macro-ing'—the ability to cross-pollinate and recognise universals.

As well as having worked in the advertising, publishing and luxury industries for many years, NET-A-PORTER co-founder Megan Quinn started a cleaning business. 'I knew nothing about cleaning,' she tells us,

in fact, I started Partners in Grime as a dare. Having been brought up in business though, I always had a very strong appreciation of the importance of customer service, loyal, energised staff, exceeding expectations, constant improvement and even humour in any business including cleaning. I took these same lessons to NET-A-PORTER. We went to enormous lengths to make our customers feel uniquely special.

Quinn knew their pure play start-up couldn't replicate in-store luxury retail experiences like handsome doormen, champagne in the changing room, and extraordinary interiors and service experiences,

We were asking people not to go into these beautiful stores and get sucky up service and stuff, how are going to get that through a computer?

So she went about reverse engineering what the customer couldn't get in-store, and layered that with exemplary customer service and designed the now iconic packaging.

Quinn is a master of macro-ing and mixing. 'Macro-ing' is the ability to identify, replicate and apply big themes and concepts to multiple situations and jurisdictions and 'mixing' is the ability to blend different skills, inputs and ideas from multiple sources into coherent new ideas.

Former Viacom co-president and MTV founder Tom Freston made a similar observation: 'Innovation is taking two things that already exist and putting them together in a new way.'

So how might we exercise our mixing and macro-ing muscles?

3 BE BROADLY INTERESTED AND PRODIGIOUSLY CURIOUS

Steve Jobs had a casual interest in calligraphy, which he indulged while hanging around Reed College campus as a college drop out. This contributed enormously to the variety of fonts we now enjoy in word processing and presentation software. At the time, the connection and usefulness of such an interest was not immediately apparent and yet it's something we now take for granted.

In much the same way, George de Mestral didn't start life as an entrepreneur, but as an electrical engineer who enjoyed the outdoors. But while he was out for a hike one day, his curiosity was piqued upon noticing the burrs sticking to his trousers.

When he got home he took a closer look under a microscope. He noticed how the burrs were made of tiny hooks, an effect he thought he could replicate using artificial materials. This simple act of curiosity led to the creation of Velcro (and the Velcro Company), an invention that is sold all over the world and brings in revenue of around $100 million every year.

However, de Mestral's journey was not as simple as it plays out in a short, two-paragraph retelling. It took years for his invention to come to fruition. But his curiosity was the catalyst for his breakthrough innovation, which, every day, saves many parents from tears and tantrums due to shoes being 'too tight' or 'un-tie-able'!

This capacity to draw from broad experiences goes well beyond undermining the shoelace and zipper industries.

Conceptual breakthroughs, a form of inductive reasoning, occur because you see a relationship that was not seen before. So how does that happen? We believe that often, the stimulus for a conceptual breakthrough is an analogous experience.

For most of us, our education and skill set tend to go deep and narrow, and this lack of 'unrelated stimulus' can actually limit our creativity.

If you, like us, are a fan of the movie *Avatar*, you will not be surprised to hear that its creator, James Cameron, was a long-time fan of deep-sea diving, having become obsessed with Jacques Cousteau as a 15-year-old.

In his 2010 TED talk he shares how his love of diving had an impact on his career. Cameron tells the audience about making *Titanic* and convincing the Hollywood studios to fund his dive on the wreck (principally because he desperately wanted to see it for himself) by explaining why it would make great PR and generate column inches and ticket sales.

It was adventure, it was curiosity, it was imagination ... it was an experience Hollywood couldn't give me.

This exploration, flying a robotic vehicle underwater through the Titanic's remains, and the unique combination of Cameron's life experiences, had a fundamental influence on how *Avatar* was made:

> *It really made me realise that the telepresence experience — that you actually can have these robotic avatars, then your consciousness is injected into the vehicle, into this other form of existence.*

Curiosity allows us to gather inputs and ideas we don't expect and for 'randomness' to be strategically generated. Cultivate your curiosity. Explore widely and be interested in things outside of your direct work.

These things will make you unique and ensure that you will be the only person who can bring that exact combination to the table. (Something that will difficult for a robot to replace.)

4 GENERATE UNEXPECTED COLLISIONS

'Creativity is just connecting things,' observed Steve Jobs. 'When you ask creative people how they did something, they feel a little guilty because they didn't really do it, they just saw something.'

Very often, creativity has no relationship to origination in the truest sense of the word; rather, it is regularly found in existing ideas and thinking colliding in new and unique ways to generate fresh ways of seeing what might be right in front of us.

In fact, worrying about originality can be a distraction when it comes to creativity. The success of a creative idea is less about whether it's new or not, and more about whether it's useful (or helpful or desirable) or not.

In the execution of his job as a Russian patent clerk, Genrich Altshuller spent more time than most analysing patents — hundreds of thousands of them, in fact. One of the things he discovered (in addition to creating *teoriya resheniya izobretatelskikh zadatch* — a theory of inventive problem solving) was that the most successful commercial patents combined existing things in ways they had not been combined before.

William Ian Beardmore Beveridge, in his book *The Art of Scientific Investigation*, also observed this phenomenon: 'Originality often consists in finding connections or analogies between two or more objects or ideas not previously shown to have any bearing on each other.'

It's a theme we picked up on when we sat down to chat with Martin Mackay, the British-born regional head of Asia–Pacific for a US technology giant. Martin claims that the capacity to mix different inputs, to place unrelated ideas and people into a shared space and to vary your experiences in unexpected ways was key to his success as a leader. 'I call it the Blondie approach,' he explained, 'after the seminal album *Parallel Lines*!'

In other words, being broadly read and experienced is one thing, but we must also be open to, and in fact try to expose ourselves to, collisions between the unexpected if we are to create the unprecedented.

5 LEARN TO REPURPOSE LIKE A CHILD

To a child, any inanimate object they can lay their hands on has the potential to be anything at all. A stick can be a machine gun or a magic wand, a cardboard box a tree house or a rocket ship.

We all repurpose objects and ideas intuitively as children, but somehow this gift eludes us as we enter adulthood.

While chatting to our clever friend Brett King, a futurist, fin-tech guru and bank heretic, the topic of conversion came up.

'We have always needed conversion as a skill,' King suggested.

During the hunter-gatherer age we turned wild animals into meat. During the agrarian age we converted seed into bread and other carbohydrates, during manufacturing we converted raw resources (iron and coal) into tangible assets. We now convert information into intangible assets.

This ability to take something and wonder what else it could be used for, what else we might turn it into, is a powerful tool of creativity.

In fact, many of the business success stories that grab headlines today are prime examples of the power of conversion; taking under-utilised resources and transforming them into something useful. Consider Uber, Airbnb, Airtasker, many of the makers on Etsy, and, yes, even Tinder (it seems human beings can be under-utilised also).

∞

Conversion, reinvention and transformation are powerful tools of creativity that not only create value and utility — they help reduce waste. What's more, as robots and AI take many existing jobs that we might consider boring or unproductively time-consuming, we may find ourselves with some of those extra minutes, hours and days that futurists and sci-fi authors have been promising us for generations.

This means that conversion will also be important in terms of how we rethink and repurpose our use of time — repurposing work time into leisure, converting work from survival to personal expression, and from the traditional work week to the gig economy.

As King explained, 'As robotics and AI take many existing jobs, wealth redistribution will be less of an issue than that of how we utilise our time.'

Ultimately, we will all need to convert the way we spend our personal energy. This will require a conversion of mindset, from one of 'work to live' to some version of 'work in your passion'.

∞

Conversion is a capability that has defined human advancement throughout history. It's more than an ability to create and utilise tools; it's the ability to recognise unrealised value in people and resources and to unlock that value and activate it for commercial or social gain. It is a skill that will always be in demand, and one you would be wise to cultivate.

APPLICATION

FIVE STEPS FOR INCREASING YOUR CONVERSION CAPABILITY

1. Look for the big themes.
2. Transfer, mix and macro.
3. Be broadly interested and prodigiously curious.
4. Generate unexpected collisions.
5. Learn to repurpose like a child.

Problem solving

The thing about problem solving is, sometimes it's not until we create a new solution that we realise there was a problem in the first place.

Michael Smith is the owner of The Sun Theatre. It is a small cinema in Yarraville, a suburb in the west of Melbourne in Victoria, Australia. When he first bought The Sun, it was a dank, mouldy ruin ready for demolition. But, acting on a hunch, he invested his time, energy and a considerable amount of money in lovingly restoring the old timber cinema seats and the artfully decorated foyer. Just so we're clear, he didn't update the cinema to conventional modern standards, but rather to its original condition from in its heyday.

It didn't make sense. It was expensive. Uncertain. *Risky!*

In a world where big chain cinemas dominate the industry with a model designed around Saturday nights (the biggest movie-going night by far), where they cram people in and run as many ads as they can before people will walk out, this looked like madness.

We did none of that. We put in the most amazing chairs we could. We run no ads. We choose the films we show and we serve the community and the customer first ... always!

'For instance,' Smith continued,

> The Secret Life of Pets *was launching and the team and I were brainstorming ideas on how we could do something creative with it. We came up with the idea of letting people watch the movie accompanied by their pets.*

Of course, there is an inherent problem with having animals indoors for a 90-minute session, as you may have already guessed. But where most people would look for all the reasons why they *couldn't* do something, Smith and his team embraced the problem and looked for reasons and ways they could.

> *The thing that would have stopped every other cinema in the country (and perhaps the world) was that the pets might relieve themselves on the carpet or on the chair. But that was worst-case. So what would we do if that happened? We realised we would have to clean the carpet. Something we do anyway. They're constantly being stained with wine, beer, soft drinks, ice cream anyway!*

This *problem solving* mindset permeates Smith's business.

In fact, unconsciously, or perhaps a little consciously, Mike was solving a problem the broader cinema industry didn't even realise it had; that of repeat business, weight of sale and frequency of interaction with their customers.

'The big chains have an average of four visits a year from their customers. We have 16.'

Not only are Smith's customers loyal, but the cinema punches far above its weight on the fame front too. After hearing about the lengths The Sun had gone to for the premiere of *The Hateful Eight*, Quentin Tarantino, Samuel L Jackson and Kurt Russell crashed the launch and did an impromptu Q & A with the audience.

Unsurprisingly, Smith is also the kind of person whose story should be up on the big screen at his own theatre. In 2016, Smith was named Australian Adventurer of the Year after becoming the first to fly a small, amphibious plane around the world solo.

So, should we all 'be like Mike'? And if so, how?

CRITICAL FACTORS MAKING PROBLEM SOLVING A FOREVER SKILL:

- **Problems are becoming increasingly complex.**
- **Problems are where opportunities hide.**
- **The greatest impact we can make on our performance lies in our ability to solve the problems that most people are unwilling to face.**

At its core, creativity is a problem-solving skill.

Not that all creativity emerges from an awareness of a problem, but rather it is informed by a mindset of 'How could this be better?'

Creative thinkers seek to improve things. Rather than shying from challenges and roadblocks they understand that problems are the lifeblood of innovation.

If we want to be more creative, we need to be willing to shift our mindset from annoyance and frustration to curiosity.

People who improve things will always be in demand, so we can become one of them if we:

1. Learn to love problems.
2. Think in questions, not statements.
3. Look for answers, not the answer.
4. Do the work (creativity is a numbers game).
5. Fail well.

1 LEARN TO LOVE PROBLEMS

Actively seek them out!

In fact, the first problem we encounter when it comes to problem solving is finding a problem worth solving. This is rather more difficult than it sounds, as most of us have been conditioned and trained to ignore problems or else make them someone else's to solve.

One of the leadership programs that Kieran runs with an extraordinary colleague, Janine Garner, has a task in it where future leaders are asked to find a problem they are passionate about solving in their organisation. They then spend months working with Kieran and Janine to define the problem, develop the solution and create a white paper on it before presenting their solution to the board and executive leadership team in a lightning talk.

Unsurprisingly, on day one when they hear their task, there are groans and moans and resistance. However, over the course of the program, this begins to shift as they start to see the value of problem finding. They begin to see their problem as a springboard to showcase the kind of thinking they can bring to the company as a leader.

One of the participants in the program was a woman in her twenties named Sheree. She had noticed that the servers the business built were taking longer to arrive at their clients' premises than was ideal. This led her to question, 'Why?'

She discovered that before getting shipped out, each server they built had to go through a complex and drawn-out checking process. Many of them were older legacy checks, some were checks that could and should be automated, and some of them could be solved and never need to be performed again.

Her problem, and its solution, was then built around a key question, 'Who's checking the checks?' The problem wasn't driven by human error or a lack of engagement; it was simply that checks that had initially been useful had become irrelevant.

Her project has since been adopted globally and is saving the company significant quantities of time, money, client frustrations and lost sales. It has also brought Sheree to the attention of the organisation's global leadership.

An ability to solve problems will always elevate your status and usefulness in your work, so we must all cultivate this skill in ourselves.

Even in the process of solving problems, new problems and challenges along the way can actually be a good thing. In fact, we've found that the greater the restrictions we are operating under, the richer the creativity.

It's something that is evident in reality shows, of all places. *Project Runway*, for instance, always creates unnecessary constraints that contestants have to work within and it leads to better, more innovative solutions.

If, every week, they simply said, 'You have a week and an unlimited budget to do whatever you like', there would be no inherent tension, no bootstrapping creativity and the show would be pretty boring, with most contestants struggling to solve an ill-defined challenge.

But what tools and techniques can we learn to help us access our inner MacGyver?

2 THINK IN QUESTIONS, NOT STATEMENTS

The problem with thinking in statements is that they presuppose a solution. There's a big difference between the statement 'We need to build a bridge' and the question 'How might we get across a body of water?'

One approach closes off possibility, the other opens up multiple possibilities. Now, many of these possibilities will be impractical and unworkable. Few people will want to be shot out of a cannon into a waiting safety net, or sign up for an Evel Knievel–themed motorcycle taxi service, but when your choice is limited to one option, it's not really a choice at all.

We need to teach ourselves, our teams and our kids to turn statements into questions when they are problem solving. This actively forces our brain to consider different solutions and look for connections it otherwise wouldn't.

Questions change the parameters in which we operate.

When we make statements we get the answers we expect. For example, in 2012, Houston Airport had a high number of complaints about the time it took for bags to reach the carousels for collection. The customers hated waiting (unsurprisingly) and expressed their discontent.

Traditional statement-based thinking would say, 'In order to reduce customer complaints we need to speed up baggage delivery.' Yet if we reframe the problem as a question such as 'How can we reduce wait times?' different solutions emerge.

In the end, the solution they implemented was to move the carousels further away from the arrival gates so that passengers' bags could make it to the carousels faster than the passengers could on foot. In other words, the solution wasn't faster delivery; it was altering the perception of time.

The point is, you will only get alternative answers and solutions if you have a methodology allowing those solutions to reveal themselves. A skill you would be wise to cultivate.

3 LOOK FOR ANSWERS, NOT THE ANSWER

Most of our time in school is spent in pursuit of the *right answer*. Two plus two is four. Hydrogen combined with oxygen in a 2:1 ratio creates water. And the words chosen by one William Shakespeare must never be questioned.

However, rarely is life so definitive, and seldom is there a single right answer to more complicated problems.

This has always been true. But the complex problems and interconnected challenges we face in the modern world have made our capacity to generate *answers* (plural), rather than just the right answer, incredibly important.

Truthfully, there is always more than a single solution to any problem we face, and allowing ourselves to explore multiple options can relieve much of the panic and pressure we experience around problem solving. It also allows us to reach conclusions that might otherwise elude us.

One of the reasons this is so important is that the human brain looks for patterns and tends to bias towards short cuts. This means if we have already found one way to solve a problem, we become resistant to the idea of searching for alternatives.

In our experience, having run and lectured at Australasia's premier creative school and delivered hundreds of guided innovation programs for industries in just about every business sector, people tend to fall in love with their second or third idea.

Of course, we're willing to admit that our first idea is probably not so great. Then we have a second idea. 'Not bad', we'll put that one to the side as the idea to beat. Then, when our third idea is as underwhelming as the first, that second idea starts to look like an act of genius.

Of course, our second ideas might indeed be genius, but we've clearly tested very little of the available creativity or opportunity we have at our disposal.

This essentially means that we have a narrow pool to choose from — much like dating in a small rural town compared to a big city. Cue sinister-sounding banjos.

To be truly creative, to generate ideas and innovations that we have not seen before, we must be willing to go further than expected, to push beyond idea number three to idea number ten, 100 or even 10 000.

In the end, becoming a better problem solver, lifting your creative capabilities, is a numbers game!

4 DO THE WORK (CREATIVITY IS A NUMBERS GAME)

Albert Einstein once observed, 'It's not that I am so smart it's just that I stay with problems longer than you.'

Put simply, the secret of problem solving is effort. Our own mental laziness is perhaps the greatest barrier to reaping the rewards of creativity.

When new recruits begin their careers in the creative industries, they are encouraged to adopt a ferocious work ethic with motivational quotes such as, 'Greatness comes at 2 am slumped over your drawing board'. (We're pretty sure the first iteration of this quote mentioned 11 pm. Such is the nature of competitive inflation!)

Don Schlitz is a Grammy-winning American songwriter who's in the Nashville Hall of Fame. In a 2018 interview conducted by the Library of Congress, he tells the story of learning to write songs. Bob McDill, 'one of the premiere songwriters', told him, 'You will get ten songs a year from inspiration but your job is to write 40 or more songs that can get on the radio.' Schlitz took that to heart.

Former paratrooper platoon commander Bradley Trevor Greive has sold over 30 million books in over 115 countries. He also understands the power of creative effort:

> *I was always passionate about writing and illustrating but following my truncated military career, when I turned professional, I applied far greater discipline to my creative endeavours and it yielded far greater results than merely being creative whenever the mood took me.*

Greive adds,

> *Creative discipline seems painfully obvious now, but at the time it was transformative. The next big step forward for me was applying creative thinking to every aspect of my life — when not having enough time or money to do something is merely the start of a problem-solving exercise, suddenly anything is possible. There is a wonderful expression, a neat paraphrasing of Erwin Rommel, that is popular in the paratroopers and goes like this, 'Sweat saves blood and brains save sweat.'*

If we paraphrase Greive and Rommel a little here, a more universal expression might be made by swapping 'blood' for 'time' or 'money'.

As we're digesting this wisdom, another thought occurs to Greive:

> *I happily agree that good ideas can come from anywhere, and indeed anyone, however great ideas most often come from people who consistently apply themselves to creative thinking while also immersing themselves in the problem at hand and actively seeking inspiration by investigating many different fields. It's not magic, it's just hard work.*

To be truly creative, to generate solutions beyond the obvious or expected, we must commit to working harder at problem solving than most people are willing to.

More than hard work and diligent effort, we must also be willing to execute.

5 FAIL WELL

You've probably heard motivational speakers, evangelists of the New Thought movement and quoters of clichés tell you, 'There's no such thing as failure.'

This is demonstrably not true. Not only is failure a real thing, it's not always necessarily a bad thing!

Having said that, it is important to note that failing exactly the same way over and over and over again is absolutely not a good thing. It is in fact, *failing badly*.

Failing badly is characterised by not learning, not changing or not even being willing to try something new to execute a new strategy.

FAIL!

Let's not do that. We can do better than that.

Scientists, by contrast, actually file and label their failures in folders so that others might more easily find them and learn from them.

This is the kind of thinking we should bring to failing well. It's useful to think of failing not in terms of finality, but as the next step in the process. It's simply a new problem to solve. While this can obviously be disappointing, it does align with our view that creativity is an ongoing and iterative process. A failure in systems or design or application might then be thought of as the next part of the creative process.

Creativity requires constant adjustment, a willingness to fail and to try a new approach. WD40 (a favourite of dads around the world) is named for its iteration in the learning curve — it's Water Displacement formula number 40. How many organisations today would be willing to admit to 39 failures *in their name*?

Angry Birds was famously the developers' 103rd attempt to create a killer app. Rather than seeing the initial lack of engagement as a failure, they considered it as part of a continuum. Failure wasn't fatal, it was simply the next challenge or problem to be met and solved.

To fail well, we must be willing to embrace all of our failure in order that we might learn from it.

One of the most famous and fortunate accidents of the twentieth century is the discovery of penicillin. Alexander Fleming failed to clean up his work area before going on vacation one day in 1928. Upon returning, Fleming noticed that there was a strange fungus on some of his cultures. Even more peculiar was that bacteria didn't seem to thrive near those cultures.

With some experiential insight, a creative reframe and more experiments to test his hypothesis, what he discovered was that in his failure (and lack of general hygiene) were the elements of an outstanding success.

This fungus became the first antibiotic, and it's still one of the most widely used antibiotics. To think this great discovery might have fallen victim to failing badly and been quickly scrubbed away while Fleming muttered angrily to himself that he must remember to clean up before he goes away in the future.

The title of this book is *Forever Skills*, however, in researching this subject we've also found it useful to identify forever challenges. Put simply, rather than focusing purely on abilities, or capabilities or character traits, it's also important to identify what issues we will face in the future and where value will always be needed. This makes problem solving a critical Forever Skill.

FIVE STEPS FOR BECOMING A BETTER PROBLEM SOLVER

1. Learn to love problems.
2. Think in questions, not statements.
3. Look for answers, not the answer.
4. Do the work (creativity is a numbers game).
5. Fail well.

Agility

Despite the many clichés surrounding Darwin's work, it is not the strongest who survive, but rather the most adaptable.

Layne Beachley is an *eight-time* world champion surfer. It would be fair to call Layne a living legend.

When we sat down to talk with Layne, she outlined her belief in the importance of adaptability and agility in high performance. She shared with us the story of getting to number two in the world and then having to relearn one of the most basic skills in surfing: how to stand up on her board!

> *The way I was doing it enabled me to reach number two but it wasn't going to get me to number one, and I wanted to be number one! It meant I had to relearn something I had been doing since I started surfing as a 4 year old. To achieve that, I had to practice jumping to my feet prior to every surf and every competitive heat for a whole year!*

Extreme? Perhaps, but that willingness to relearn and create something new is a creative agility skill that many high achievers and great leaders have in common.

Becoming great, becoming a world champion, is not just about how good we are, but also how willing we are to adapt, learn something new and even start over again.

What can get in the way of this agility and adaptability, as explained in chapter 1, is that we are pretty much wired to resist change.

That being said, versatility and a willingness to be flexible in our approach has always been critical in setting human beings up for success. Our ability to adapt to new environmental conditions; rethink our capacity to defend ourselves, as weapons and threats became more lethal and closer to hand; and to adopt new technology in the pursuit of improved living standards and health are all hallmarks of the success of our species.

It may not necessarily feel natural or comfortable to push ourselves to try the unfamiliar, but learning to operate in the space of 'non-lethal discomfort' is a necessary skill if we are to future-proof ourselves and those around us.

CRITICAL FACTORS MAKING AGILITY A FOREVER SKILL:

- **The path to success is rarely a straight line.**
- **Few endeavours are successful in their first iteration.**
- **Resilience is not trying a failed strategy repeatedly, but rather trying a new approach with optimism.**

The parameters, environment and challenges we find ourselves facing today, and that we will face in the future, will constantly change. This means we too must start to see change as the constant that Heraclitus promised.

In fact, those who adapt, who create new ways of doing things and persevere from 'one failure to the next without losing enthusiasm', as Winston Churchill encouraged us, are the ones who have traditionally thrived throughout history.

To become more agile, more adaptable, more capable and skilful in the face of change, we must be willing to advance our thinking, or indeed, *rethink* our thinking, beliefs and behaviours.

Rethinking requires discipline, focus and a willingness to challenge our own points of view and existing mindset. But if change is going to remain a forever challenge, then agility of thought will also be a Forever Skill.

To foster agility, we must:

1. Think of resilience as mental agility.

2. Imagine an alternative framework or universe.

3. Push beyond 'the obvious barrier'.

4. Challenge our own assumptions.

5. Develop multiple senses of awareness.

1 THINK OF RESILIENCE AS MENTAL AGILITY

In the hundreds of conversations and interviews we've conducted around this concept of Forever Skills, 'resilience' is one of those words that came up time and time again as a defining factor of success.

Interestingly, the definitions and meanings that people attach to this seemingly simple word are remarkably varied.

Some define resilience as mental toughness, best served with a cup of concrete and a 'harden up' attitude. However, on digging in a little further, most people tended to moderate and broaden their views of resilience and associate it more with mental flexibility, adaptability and the ability to 'bounce back' after a challenge.

In other words, resilience is, at its heart, a creative skill, and crucial to agility. We need to shift our conception of resilience from 'running at the same impenetrable wall without losing enthusiasm' to one of applying that enthusiasm to trying a new approach every time. Can't break through the wall? Build a door. Open a window. Buy a ladder. Rent a crane with a wrecking ball!

In her keynote speaking and team training, Kieran often talks about the '6 R's of Resilience':

1. reframe

2. regroup

3. rethink

4. rework

5. reward

6. reinforce.

We need to be more mentally agile in:

1. how we interpret a challenge (reframe)

2. how we collaborate and coordinate with our team and network (regroup)

3. the strategies we decide to put in place (rethink)

4. being iterative in the approach we implement (rework)

5. acknowledging progress (reward)

6. measuring and maintaining progress (reinforce).

Resilience—turning adversity into something useful—also requires creating a more helpful meaning for what reality decides to hand us. While we cannot always control what happens, we can become more agile in how we respond and move forward when life throws us grenades. This is perhaps the most critical use of mental agility. It's something people who survive great trauma often talk about.

Recently, we met an inspiring young man who had just launched a charity raising money for childhood victims of burns, and he wanted to sell us a calendar. Fuelled with another skill critical to creativity, curiosity, we got talking about why he was doing what he was doing.

He explained that he was the victim of a violent sexual assault that he barely made it through. He was subsequently harassed and bullied, and anonymously encouraged that the world would be better without him.

We discovered that what had got him through was a capacity to turn this trauma into something useful, to see this brutal crime as a chance to leave his current circumstance and re-create his life. So he decided to do something to help others.

Creativity isn't just about creating things, it is also the ability to create a new mindset or reframe a world view in a way that is helpful rather than a hindrance. Agility is far more than a physical or cognitive function; it also applies to our emotions and our beliefs systems.

Chris Helder is a very wise (and ridiculously high-energy) friend of ours. Chris has often talked with us about a powerful concept outlined in his book, *Useful Belief*:

> *I don't teach positive, I teach useful. I don't think truth matters as much as we think it really does. You'll find truth is very much a perception anyway; we've often let other people create our truths.*

Chris went on to tell us that we might as well move our mental frame and choose a belief that is useful to the consequences we're seeking. While Chris does not necessarily refer to his idea this way, useful belief is very much a creative tool.

Essentially he helps leaders, organisations and teams be agile and invent new meaning that is more conducive to a favourable outcome.

Resilience is ultimately about being flexible and open-minded in how we frame our challenges, think about them, act upon them and receive feedback from them.

This makes our capacity to be mentally agile critical.

2 IMAGINE AN ALTERNATIVE FRAMEWORK OR UNIVERSE

In the movie *Dead Poets Society*, Robin Williams's character encourages all of his students to climb onto their desks so that they might see the room, and their world, differently.

It's something we teach leaders, teams and organisations to do using a methodology called Impossible Thinking™, a technique that was instrumental in helping us name our own business, The Impossible Institute.

We were inspired by our experience of high school mathematics (words that we're quite sure have never been used in quite this order before ... ever).

In high school, we are all initially taught that you cannot take the square root of a negative number. It's a rule that makes logical sense to even the least interested pre-teen.

Then one day, a couple of years later, our mathematics teacher decides to play 'let's pretend'. Yes, even in mathematics, creativity techniques such as make believe have a role.

What we come to accept is that the square root of a negative number (-1) has an imaginary value called i (or j if you're studying electrical engineering). With this simple suspension of belief, an entire branch of complex mathematics opens up and calculations that were once impossible suddenly become possible.

In other words, by imagining an alternative framework or universe, being agile in terms of how we think and what we choose to believe, we are able to explore what lies on the other side of 'impossible' and then work backwards to our current position.

We used this method with a large financial services company as part of a strategic workshop and innovation program.

One of the key issues they faced was that, as an organisation of significant scale and with a huge client base, their customers were becoming angry and frustrated whenever they were placed on hold after calling the contact centre. During their 'on hold' experience, they'd become so riled up that by the time they actually spoke to someone, they were in no mood to be nice or even pleasant.

This not only meant they might decide take their business elsewhere, but their staff were also constantly having to engage with extremely unhappy customers. This made for a less-than-ideal work environment, rising disengagement and high staff turnover.

They had initially contacted us to help them run a training program to drive performance and efficiency in their team, in an effort to help them get customers on and off the line more swiftly (a strategy hardly conducive to customer or staff satisfaction).

Instead, we introduced them to Impossible Thinking™, and asked, 'What would it take for customers to *want* to be placed on hold?'

The options that opened up have been inspired. We have explored a partnership with a record label, where their stable of artists will record unplugged versions of songs that can *only* be heard in this organisation's on-hold playlist. It's possible that people who aren't even customers will call up and demand to be put on hold.

Another opportunity we explored involved gamifying the on-hold experience so that clients and customers can earn rewards based on the time they have spent waiting.

The point is, until we unlocked the agility and flexibility in their team, they could only see their challenges as single-solution problems. This is far from unusual, as we experience this phenomenon with organisations we work with around the world and from virtually every industry category.

Agility, an ability to be flexible, adaptable and resilient, is in the end a numbers game. How often can you lift yourself up and try a new approach?

3 PUSH BEYOND 'THE OBVIOUS BARRIER'

One of the greatest barriers to creativity is our brain itself. Again, this is a function of our mind working as a pattern-making machine that runs simple software based on: Learn. Repeat. Repeat. Repeat.

We like to use the example of *Family Feud* to demonstrate the power of our brain's pattern-making capabilities. *Family Feud* is ultimately a game that relies on our minds being able to generate expected answers.

Odds are, if we ask you to name something with a hole in it, you would say, 'Donut'. You might even feel a flash of pride in that moment as the host announces you have identified the 'Top answer!'

However, what 'Top answer' really means is *the most commonly thought-of answer*. It's actually not that clever at all, merely an instinctual answer based on the most common neural connection. It's the answer most likely to be our brain's default unconscious thought.

We call this 'The Obvious Barrier', for obvious reasons. To be more creative and agile, we need to develop the ability to move beyond it.

Great thinkers do this constantly. They question things. They push beyond the expected. They don't stop at or immediately accept the obvious answer. They're unsatisfied with what has been done before.

Fundamentally, they're willing to question what they believe.

4 CHALLENGE YOUR OWN ASSUMPTIONS

This phenomenon of reflexively reaching for the obvious answer also explains why, despite the inherent commercial danger of being just like everyone else, we tend to design businesses that look remarkably similar to those of our competitors.

It's why hairdressers use scissors in their signage, or why businesses with an environmental or sustainability focus choose green or hessian to feature in their packaging or professional livery. It may be because you look at that logo and think, 'It just seems so right'. Of course it seems right — you've seen hundreds just like it, usually adorning the premises of your immediate competition!

One of Britain's most innovative chefs, Heston Blumenthal, is known for his creative menus. However, his creativity and mental agility is not limited to the food he prepares or the methods he uses. He is also a wonderfully creative thinker as shown in his 2011 television series *Heston's Mission Impossible*.

In one of our favourite episodes he faces the daunting task of feeding people on a Royal Navy submarine, *HMS Turbulent*. His mission, as he has clearly chosen to accept, is to improve the quality of the food served on board and in the process lift the health and happiness of the serving crew.

The genius of Blumenthal's solution involved more than throwing a few recipes at a group of submariners with unsophisticated palates; it required completely rethinking how the food was prepared, stored, and then cooked and served.

He was able to lengthen the freshness of the produce by vacuum-sealing it and then preparing the food using sous-vide (which sounds so much better than 'giving it a gentle boil in a bag'). This not only led to superior-tasting food, but it also reduced the space required for food storage, meaning that the Royal Navy was able to store more food on board and stay at sea for longer periods.

It's not often the military capability of a nuclear sub is revolutionised in the galley. Heston challenged the assumptions of the Navy and even of himself, and so must we.

Too often, a failure to challenge base assumption is the primary barrier to agility. We default to habitual thinking and solutions based in precedent and get stuck, rather than enabling more agile thinking.

One of the assumptions that can get in the way of reacting with agility is that 'our best people need to be working on the project'. The problem, of course, is that your 'best people' may not be your best innovators. This is principally because they love the system; they thrive in the status quo. Enlisting them to innovate is akin to asking them to undermine their own success. Not easy.

Rather, it is those willing to challenge their own assumptions, and ours, that will find themselves future-proof and agile in the face of change.

5 DEVELOP MULTIPLE SENSES OF AWARENESS

'When all you have is a hammer, everything begins to look like a nail.' In other words, we all tend to rely pretty heavily on one or two tools for solving problems. And in an age of unprecedented change, this just won't do. We must broaden our sensory awareness so that we become cognisant of input we might be missing, and are better able to react with agility.

This means being agile enough to involve multiple senses and engage multiple awarenesses, from our five senses to body language, intuition, observation and understanding.

We use a methodology in our workshops and training to encourage observations in the gaps. We call it 'mine the gaps' (see figure 5.1). It involves listening to what people say they do and observing what they actually do. In the middle there is usually a gap, and it is in this gap that the real juice and power usually is. If you can close it you can be agile enough to create ideas people want and will actually use.

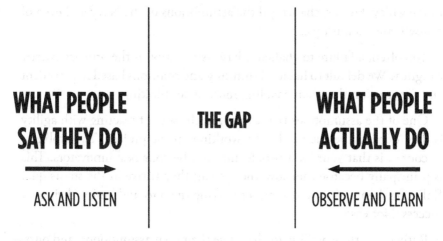

Figure 5.1 mine the gap

The identification of this gap relies on multiple inputs. You have to hear what people say (and notice what they don't), and understand why they say it. Then you must carefully observe what they do and how they do it.

The Lucky Iron Fish company is a great example of the power of this thinking. The company distributes iron fish in Cambodia, which are used in cooking to treat iron deficiencies. Iron can be transferred fairly effectively from iron pots, but the cost of so many pots was prohibitive. Instead, the company decided to make round iron discs to be added to cooking pots, and gave them out. While people said they would use them, no-one did (apart from as bookends or doorstops, it seemed). So the team, led by Christopher Charles, went to talk to the elders about the lucky customs around food. In doing so they discovered a fish that was thought to bring great luck and fortune. They then shaped the iron into lucky fish that you added to your pot when cooking, and adoption skyrocketed. As Charles says, 'You can have the best treatment in the world, but if people won't use it, it won't matter.'

Identifying this gap means really listening. Oscar Trimboli is an expert in deep listening and the author of the book by the same name. His work centres around the fact that information is being 'broadcast' at us constantly, while our understanding is diminishing.

'The context of what is being said is as critical as anything someone says,' Oscar explains. 'Words are just ingredients, we also need a recipe in order to make sense of all the words.'

What much of Oscar's work focuses on is shifting the idea of communications from what is said towards what is understood (a topic we pick up on in part II). The real lesson in Trimboli's work is to become more sensorily intelligent, to not only rely on one source of information, or one style of communication — to be as agile and adaptable in how we collect our input as we are in how we generate output.

While there is some dispute about the theory of sensory biases in education, what is undeniable is the fact that we all have preferences for how we receive and interpret information. The evidence is all around us, with communication via text, tweet and instant messaging showing the potential for misinterpretation is enormous (and at times hilarious, if you read Twitter SMS fails).

We have evolved to experience the world through all of our senses: visual, auditory, touch, taste and smell. Each of these senses gives us a different perspective on what we are facing and allows us to develop nuances in our understanding.

∞

Our ability to be more mentally agile is a Forever Skill. Mental agility allows us to reframe our thinking, responses, defaults, assumptions and senses and come up with more powerful solutions and options. Agility allows us to move forward when we hit a block, to rethink when we have no answer and to reimagine when hope seems lost. Skills we will all be better for having.

FIVE STEPS FOR BEING MORE AGILE

1. Think of resilience as mental agility.
2. Imagine an alternative framework or universe.
3. Push beyond 'The Obvious Barrier'.
4. Challenge your own assumptions.
5. Develop multiple senses of awareness.

PART 2

COMMUNICATION SKILLS

'IF I WENT TO COLLEGE AGAIN, I'D CONCENTRATE ON TWO AREAS: LEARNING TO WRITE AND TO SPEAK BEFORE AN AUDIENCE. NOTHING IN LIFE IS MORE IMPORTANT THAN THE ABILITY TO COMMUNICATE EFFECTIVELY.'

Gerald R Ford

The second cluster of Forever Skills is formed around what we're broadly referring to as 'communication skills'. These include such capabilities as influence, engagement, sales, presentation, leadership and other abilities that are often described as the 'soft skills'.

Rather unfairly.

The term 'soft skills' is an unhelpful hangover from the 'hard skills' biases of previous industrial revolutions. Essentially, 'hard skills' meant working with machines whereas 'soft' meant 'not machine-related'. In retrospect, calling them 'soft' can appear to undervalue their importance relative to the 'hard' or technical ones. They are not, however, less crucial, easier to attain or less impactful.

Quite the opposite.

The ability to understand human drivers and communicate powerfully has altered history. Words well chosen and well spoken have rallied communities, elevated leaders, built empires and shifted beliefs. Imagine if Martin Luther King Jr had 'a few thoughts that might be kind of handy', John F Kennedy had thought 'it might be fun if we looked into the possibility of going to the moon sometime sooner or later because we just might be able to do it', or Nike had told us to 'Make our best attempt'. A capacity to understand human motivation and apply this is clearly a key element of leadership.

These so-called 'soft' skills have helped change history and will continue to do so, and thankfully that's something we are finally waking up to. Because the experience and capabilities that matter most today are coming less and less from the world of hard skills and technical ability, and more from the world of human understanding and engagement.

In an article published in the *Australian Financial Review* in March 2018, journalist Mark Eggleton quotes LinkedIn's managing director for Australia and New Zealand, Matt Tindale, as observing that 'So-called soft skills are those that should be *baked into every employee* in the digital economy.' (Emphasis ours.)

Matt also argued at a roundtable co-hosted by *The Australian Financial Review* and DeakinCo. (a leadership development organisation aligned with Deakin University) that the demand today is for collaboration, teamwork, EQ, critical thinking and problem-solving skills. These skills, he said, are important because they are 'enterprise-transferable'. A phrase we predict you're going to hear a lot in the future.

Likewise, in October 2018, LinkedIn's global CEO Jeff Weiner, who can probably get his hands on a greater quantity of employment information (and with greater detail and data-backed accuracy) than any national government, was quoted by Simone Stolzoff in *Quartz at Work* as stating, 'The biggest skills gap in the United States is soft skills. What most employers want are written communication, oral communication, team-building, and leadership skills.'

Our own research backs that up. Every one of the people we sat down with referred to at least one of these skills as critical to their success. People also said they were the most challenging skills to learn, but the most vital when moving from a position of individual competence to one of team leadership. Scott Bales of Innovation Labs in Singapore believes in the future 'the technical skills will be able to be implanted in your brain with a chip. But the "people" skills would be forever important and differentiating'.

Crucial as people and communication skills are, perhaps because of their reputation for 'softness' they are among the least respected and understood.

The education industry deserves at least some of the blame for this. Modern educational institutions, conceived in the nineteenth century and engineered for the twentieth, have tended to focus on technical capability while doing little to nurture the human side of our intelligence and our individuality.

This bias to technical (and away from the 'emotional') is still worn like a badge of honour in some industries, companies and in different parts of the world.

One CEO we worked with was fond of saying, 'I don't have any time for all of this people stuff!' His attitude may have been a small and, we're sure, a non-causal reason that his team contacted us to develop a strategy to attract and retain top talent, as their turnover was decidedly higher than average for their sector. (Sarcasm absolutely intended.)

Poor communication skills and emotional ignorance are in fact among the most cited causes of workplace disengagement, staff turnover, broken relationships and a sense of isolation emerging between generations.

Conversely, an ability to read people, to understand them and to communicate with them in such a way that they become inspired, and feel understood and motivated, will be a critical inclusion in our future skills matrices, as it is becoming today.

Additionally, an economy with abundant employment options, including working for yourself (we currently have the lowest barriers to starting up in history), makes a capacity to not only sell to our customers, but also to engage those you wish to see on your team, in your corner and on your side, critical to the sustainability of your business, leadership or cause.

For these reasons and more, we've designated communication, in all of its manifestations, our second Forever Skills cluster.

Influence

Ideas without influence are impotent.

Whether you're a leader looking to create buy-in with your team, a sales or marketing team wanting to sell products or services, a change agent with a cause you want to champion in your community or a parent trying to get your kids to do pretty much anything you want them to, influence is a critical Forever Skill.

Of course, influence has always been important. Throughout history, an ability to inspire others with your ideas, to persuade them of your usefulness and garner their support has been a critical factor for success in even the smallest societal and organisational groupings.

Influence allows us to negotiate a deal on our terms, mould opinions, make social change, and build businesses and organisations that generate commercial and social value.

What's more, the importance of influence will only increase in the future as the volume of choice, information and options continues to grow.

CRITICAL FACTORS MAKING INFLUENCE A FOREVER SKILL:

- **Rarely does the best win. It is far more likely to be the most influential.**
- **Relying on facts rather than influence can actually be counterproductive.**
- **If you can't engage, you really can't lead.**

One of the problems we've discovered in working with smart people is that many of them would rather be right than win, or, phrased another way, they'd rather be right than rich. We become so enamoured with our own rightness that it becomes self-righteousness and costs us the very thing we desire … impact and engagement!

Often times, these smart people will complain, 'But I shouldn't have to sell … because I'm right/I have evidence/the facts are right!' Which is not to say that we shouldn't be right or that we shouldn't be passionate about our work and its efficacy. What we're really saying is 'Right is not nearly enough.' You need to build buy-in. You need to learn to influence.

Additionally, if our work, cause or ideas are important enough to us and will make a significant contribution to our community, perhaps we should really be willing to lose a little pride and learn how to sell and create engagement around them.

This is key. The downfall of many people, businesses or products is due to the lack of influence skills (and not flaws in the people, companies or products themselves).

Despite what our egos would like to believe, rarely does the best product or service dominate its category, nor does the most qualified candidate get the job (or win the election). Plus, innovative and thoughtful ideas seem to fail with alarming regularity.

Rather, the people and ideas that do succeed are those that harness the power of influence. They focus that influence in the direction of their vision.

This is especially true for leaders. Leadership is defined by many skills and attributes, from vision-setting to managing resources (including people), but ultimately, leadership's primary function is to inspire others to take action.

Put simply: to lead you must be able to generate influence.

These skills, tools and techniques can help us increase our influence:

1. Know what you're really 'selling'.

2. Align your value with their values.

3. Demonstrate who you help them to be.

4. Develop your emotional intelligence.

5. Share your ideas, values and instructions through stories.

1 KNOW WHAT YOU'RE REALLY 'SELLING'

First things first. You *are* in the business of selling. We all are.

If you're a parent, you're selling clean teeth, vegetables and bedtime; if you're a teacher, you're selling paying attention, working hard and the importance of knowledge; if you're a leader you're selling a culture worth belonging to, work worth doing and yourself as someone worth following. This will never change. As long as there are people to connect with there will be the need to persuade and sell.

Yet most people don't like to think they have to sell, let alone understand what they're truly selling. Even those in sales!

This is partly due to the fact that, in every sale, presentation, pitch, political campaign or one-to-one conversation, there are multiple levels of engagement and selling at play. We call this the 'Selling Stack' (see figure 6.1, overleaf).

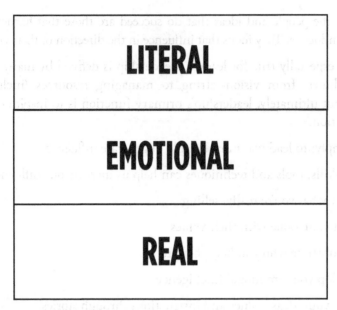

Figure 6.1 the Selling Stack™

At the top level is the literal or tangible level of the sale. It's the product or service you provide, expressed in the most simple and everyday terms.

Beneath that, at the second level of the Selling Stack, is where you'll locate the emotional component of the sale. This is informed by how buying the product or joining the cause will make us feel. Does it make us feel safe, or savvy, or even superior? This is where most salespeople try to play, shifting a prospect's focus from features to benefits.

Sitting at the base of the Selling Stack is the real, the actual or psychological level of the sale. This is what people are truly buying, and where extraordinary influence is to be found. Now, an overt description of this level of the sale might never be expressed out loud, put down on paper or communicated on a website, but an understanding of it should inform all of our communications.

So what does this look like in a real-world example?

Some years ago we were working with an entrepreneur incubator helping a few hundred entrepreneurs develop their business strategies.

One of the people in the room was Nick Peardon. Nick is a young arborist based in Melbourne, Australia. He was energetic and full of ambition and enthusiasm.

We asked for a volunteer to go through the process of the Selling Stack live on stage. Nick, as we mentioned, was leaking enthusiasm and immediately volunteered.

When we asked Nick what he thought he was really selling, he responded, 'I help people feel good about cutting down trees!'

Somewhat predictably, the audience burst out laughing, and we kindly suggested that this was probably not something he should put on his website.

When we probed further, we learned Nick was actually an environmentalist. He hated the fact that the vast majority of trees, once cut down, were chipped and turned into garden mulch. 'Not only is this wasteful,' he went on to explain, 'it also releases all of the stored carbon contained in the timber of the tree.'

Nick's solution to this problem was inspired. Whenever he had to remove a tree that was of a certain size, rather than chipping the timber, he kept it as whole as he could and transformed it into furniture.

The whole room instantly shared the same thought: 'That is brilliant!'

Yet this fact was so hidden on his website that only the very persistent (and possibly Nick's mum) would ever find it. It would never do.

Within the next ten minutes, we had renamed Nick's business as Treeincarnation, registered the URL and developed a sales and marketing strategy for Nick based on the Selling Stack.

At the first level, the literal level, Nick was obviously selling tree removal. At the second, emotional level, his customers felt better about something that was necessary but not something they felt particularly proud of. At the third, real level, what he was actually selling, the psychological underpinning of the sale, was not tree removal — it was guilt removal.

Now, this is not something Nick will ever articulate with a customer or in the media. ('Want to feel less guilty about your environmental assault? Nick removes guilt!' Yeah, no. No-one really wants to admit to the fact that they might be driven by a sense of guilt.) However, it absolutely drives his engagement planning.

One of the sales strategies we helped Nick develop on the back of this was a campaign to approach schools in his local area after a severe weather event to take care of any fallen trees and large branches.

The value add, or special sauce, that Nick offered was a promise to take the timber and use it to build furniture for an outdoor classroom where teachers could talk to students about environmental science and sustainability.

This got people talking about tree removal in ways they didn't before.

When you know what you're really selling, or offering, or delivering, your influence amplifies.

2 ALIGN YOUR VALUE WITH THEIR VALUES

To find true engagement (or a sale, or follower-ship or buy-in), we must always look to the other side of the table. But often, we're so focused on our ideas, products and agendas that we lose sight of the other side altogether and think only about ourselves.

When we try to generate influence around our ideas, products, services, ways of behaving or processes, we tend to become caught up at our end of the equation. We shouldn't.

The sale is not in the product; it is always in the prospect.

Despite this, we list features and benefits, deliver more detail than is required (after all, we invested all this time and money in our research and development so we'd better make a point of it) and spend a much-too-significant quantity of time espousing why we are the best candidate for the job, the best representative for our community, the best use of our supporter's limited charity budget or the best product on the market.

What we rarely consider is what things look like to those we wish to engage and serve — in other words, what's in it for them?

One of the things we found most interesting in our research into influence as a Forever Skill was how predictably a person's economic and social success seemed to correlate with the amount of detail they could tell us about the people they served.

High awareness equalled high engagement and success. Take Phillip Di Bella, an Australian entrepreneur who divides his time between Australia and New Zealand and is the founder of Di Bella Coffee, a premium coffee bean roaster that began in Queensland.

Just to provide some context for our international readers, who may not be familiar with Australia's geography and demography: Phil could have founded his coffee business in Melbourne, a city whose coffee obsession rivals that of the Italians (an ethnicity that also contributes significantly to Melbourne's current population), but he chose Queensland.

Again, for context, Queensland is a hot, humid state in Australia that often prides itself on its laid-back attitude — you might even say lack of sophistication. It's akin to founding a business based on nuanced flavour cues in Alabama, rather than New York, and then trying to sell that product to discerning New Yorkers!

What emerged from our interview with Phil was incredibly interesting. He doesn't consider the people who drink his coffee as his primary customer. Obviously, he cares about them and wants them to have the most extraordinary coffee experience he can provide, but Phil believes his true customers are the café and restaurant owners. Small-business people just like himself.

Phil isn't selling good coffee (well, of course he does actually sell them some amazingly high-quality coffee). What he *really* sells them is support for what they care most about: their businesses. Phil applies his focus to helping café and restaurant owners maximise the profitability of their businesses by providing business strategy, new product development, improved graphics and merchandising as well as interior design. The quid pro quo is, they exclusively buy his coffee beans at a premium price because they are buying so much more than coffee.

This is a key distinction that many people miss in their influence strategies. We often fail to realise who our real customer is and what they really want.

Here's our advice that will be useful forever: Want to know who your customer is? Follow the money. Want to know who your constituents are? Follow the votes. Want to know who's on your side? Follow the love and support.

What transformed Phil's business from a one-person start-up run by a guy sleeping on the factory floor into the international organisation it has now become was his focus on serving his *real* customers in a way none of his competitors had.

In other words, he focused on what they cared most about and framed his value in terms of their values!

So, if you want to increase your influence, always think: 'What's in it for them?'

3 DEMONSTRATE WHO YOU HELP THEM TO BE

All human behaviour, every choice we make, every decision we grapple with is ultimately filtered through our sense of identity. In other words, who we think we are and the image we want to project to the world.

This shows up in every part of our lives. People act out of their national identities, their gender identities, their position in the family, their professional roles and their public perceptions and aspirations.

What's critical here is that this behaviour is largely unconscious and unprompted. We develop a sense of unconscious competence around these behaviours. So much so that acting in alignment with these identities becomes virtually automatic.

Culture is a perfect example of this, whether it be national or ethnic identity, social or sporting identity or even corporate and team identity:

- People raised in East Asia find using chopsticks to eat completely intuitive.

- Sports fans become irrationally emotional and attached to the outcomes of games that they're not even playing in as participants.

- People in tech, banking and finance, the military, retail and professional services all tend to dress, speak and carry themselves in a predictable way in alignment with their particular group.

Of course these are generalisations, but the point is, much of our behaviour is codified unconsciously at an identity level.

This tendency can also have negative consequences. The issues we currently face in redefining our expectations of gender roles, sexuality and racial prejudice are anchored in some very long-held beliefs that are shaped by our cultural identities. And, as identity is often unconscious, this can be very hard to shift.

However, identity is also a critical factor in driving influence.

For example, people don't say, 'I bought a Macintosh computer' or 'I purchased some Apple hardware', but rather, prompted by Apple's very effective marketing campaigns, they are more likely to say something like 'I'm a Mac person.' And just as critically, 'I am not a PC person.'

In fact, the marketing and advertising industry has always used identity to persuade us that certain products will make us the kind of person who is cool, on trend or socially accepted. It has convinced us variously to smoke a particular brand of cigarette or quit smoking, drive one make of car over another, or make certain choices in clothing or brand of bottled water.

Politicians also invoke a sense of national pride and community identity when trying to attract supporters and voters. How often have we heard 'My fellow Americans ...' or 'It's just un-Australian ...'.

This even affects us at a community and familial level, where our sense of social identity and conformity is strongly encouraged. Sometimes very strongly. In fact, even today, one of the worst things you can hear from your family or a close friend is 'You've changed!'

So how can identity help us drive influence?

Identity is a function of multiple factors, but here is a useful mnemonic we created:

- background
- beliefs
- behaviours.

What is the *background* or context we are operating in? There's little point building a belief system or behaviours that are irrelevant to the geographical, social or technological environment we're operating in.

What do we as a group *believe* to be true, what is our internal creed or ideology and, just as importantly, what is the hierarchy of values that flow from these beliefs?

What *behaviours*, conduct, symbols and language do we use to reinforce our sense of identity and also communicate to other members of our tribe that we're one of them?

Ultimately, using identity as a tool for influence is about moving from *telling* people what to do, buy or support to *showing* them who we help them to be. Identity will always be a powerful lever you can apply to drive influence.

4 DEVELOP YOUR EMOTIONAL INTELLIGENCE

Daniel Goleman's 2005 book *Emotional Intelligence* took the commercial world by storm. All of a sudden those who defined themselves by how they felt had a reason to feel a little superior to those whose bias was towards the rational.

But despite the perceived 'softness' that was associated with words such as 'emotional' at the time (and even today if we're being completely honest), the concept of emotional intelligence (EQ) has had a powerfully transformative effect in our schools, in corporate culture, in our relationships and even in how we develop resilience and self-awareness.

In the course of our research, we found that people had multiple definitions of emotional intelligence (as was the case with many of the skills we explored). However, in pursuit of brevity and memorability, we've collapsed them down to five key applications:

1. *Rapport.* Connecting people to each other and to us rapidly.

2. *Mobility.* Communicating across cultures and social strata.

3. *Empathy.* Gaining insight beyond our own personal experience.

4. *Understanding.* Knowing what's driving behaviour and opinion.

5. *Inspiration.* Eliciting an emotional response in others.

What's reassuring about this concept of emotional intelligence is that almost everyone we spoke to believed that it was a skill that could be learned and developed. In fact, many shared stories of their own 'Road to Damascus' moments with regard to emotional intelligence.

Chip Bell, a world-renowned expert on customer loyalty and service, explained that he thought it was critical to spend time with people 'unlike yourself' and cultivate a sense of patience, tolerance and inclusion.

He added that few executives can tell you the names of the custodians and janitors they see every day in their buildings, but the leaders with the highest emotional intelligence probably can. Chip then shared with us the story of Charles Schwab CEO Walt Bettinger. In the story Bettinger is preparing for his final exam in a business strategy course. He has done well throughout the course, has studied hard and feels well prepared. When he walks into the exam the teacher hands out a single sheet of paper that is blank on both sides. The professor proceeds to tell the class that there is only one final and most important question they need to answer: 'What's the name of the lady who cleans this building?' Bettinger didn't know. He failed, but he learned one of his most important leadership lessons ever.

> *Her name was Dottie, and I did not know Dottie. I'd seen her, but I'd never taken the time to ask her name. I have tried to know the name of every Dottie I've worked with ever since.*

Emotional intelligence is knowing people, all kinds of people. If you are emotionally intelligent enough to know what makes people do the things they do and think the things they think you will always be in good stead for success.

Bothering to understand as many human beings around you as you can is a crucial skill.

Cory Muscara is an American mindfulness expert; you may have seen him on *The Dr Oz Show*, where he is a regular guest. His meditations have been shared by millions of people on the planet. He told us that anything that requires connection and compassion will not be outsourced and that having people around you who 'work with your mindset and know what is important to you' is key to success.

This is emotional intelligence in action. Great leaders, friends, teachers and colleagues do just this. They are able to use emotional intelligence to influence others and bring out the best in them. They see who we are and who we can be and move us towards our best or better selves. Learning to be emotionally intelligent, to see what makes people their best is not only useful, but a skill the world needs more of.

In other words, periodically shift your focus outside yourself, your industry and your particular view of the world and expand your emotional palate if you want greater influence. Our ability to not simply feel emotion, but to read it and understand it, helps us build stronger connections with those around us and with those we wish to influence.

5 SHARE YOUR IDEAS, VALUES AND INSTRUCTIONS THROUGH STORIES

Stories are one of the most ancient forms of human communication we have access to and a powerful means of influencing.

Now, while it may be true that artificial intelligence can be programmed to recognise patterns in popular stories and then generate stories of its own, what is extremely hard to replicate through AI is the human capacity to engage others through shared personal stories based on experience.

Alastair Clarkson, a four-time premiership-winning Australian Football League (AFL) coach, explained this in an interview on the Fox Footy Channel's *On the Mark* program. When one of the hosts, Kelli Underwood, suggested that Clarkson had a reputation for being a storytelling coach, Clarkson responded:

> *I try to tell them stories, anecdotes of my upbringing, my childhood, my vulnerabilities and my shame to try to make it as normal as I possibly can, so they can tell their stories to me …*

Clarkson is essentially trying to use storytelling to create a good environment where his players can prosper as human beings as well as footballers. What's clear in Clarkson's response is that he's not only using stories to inspire, inform and lead, but also as a way of creating feedback opportunities that are personal, impactful and routine.

However, we can often overlook the power of stories in our communication and influence strategies. Perhaps because we first encountered stories in our childhood. Or because we're so familiar with stories, we tend to think of storytelling as so simple that we often don't consider it a skill. In fact, the template is relatively simple and has been duplicated and copied throughout the ages.

There's a beginning, a middle and an end, with a moral or lesson to be drawn out at the conclusion.

More nuanced story formulas have also been explored in classic narrative structures such as the Hero's Journey, which was articulated so brilliantly by Joseph Campbell. The formula plays out like this:

- ordinary world
- call to adventure
- refusal of the call
- meeting the mentor
- crossing the threshold
- tests, allies and enemies
- approach to the inmost cave
- ordeal
- reward (seizing the sword)
- the road back
- resurrection
- return with the elixir.

This famous formula has either directly or intuitively informed virtually every novel, stage play and movie you have likely ever seen. However, you don't need to be a screenwriter or William Shakespeare to use storytelling to amplify your influence.

We spoke to one of the world's leading authorities on business storytelling, Gabrielle Dolan, who has taught business storytelling to organisations and educational institutions around the world. We wanted to get a sense of how she sees storytelling as a tool of influence.

Dolan explained, 'Storytelling helps you engage and connect with colleagues and clients, whether you need to implement a new strategy, values or vision, kick-start or re-energise a team.'

Storytelling also helps us to codify all of the tools that inform the Forever Skill of influence.

Stories help us:

- communicate what we are really selling
- align ourselves with the values of those we serve
- provide examples of what our cultural identities look like in terms of behaviour in an emotional and engaging way
- move people emotionally in ways that don't always make logical sense.

Because of this emotional richness and connection, stories are easy to learn from.

Take for example the story of Air New Zealand's former CEO Ralph Norris. Legend has it that he was on a flight that was understaffed — one of the crew was ill. Seeing that the crew were struggling to get their service done, he got out of his seat and went to help out.

He served his customers meals. Importantly, he also served his team, his company and his brand as a leader.

Most critically, storytelling allows our ideas to be passed on and passed down and our influence to be amplified.

∞

Influence will always be required if we are to give life to our ideas and thinking. In part I, we explained the importance of creativity: generating better ideas, more innovative solutions and greater agility in our approach to the challenges we face in business and in life. What has also become apparent in our research is that a capacity to build influence around these ideas, solutions and approaches is just as important, if not more so. Likewise for leaders: if we cannot generate enrolment and buy-in and move others towards a common goal we never realise our potential. Many great ideas and people fail, not because they are flawed but because they are not bought into.

Put bluntly, ideas and people without influence are impotent.

APPLICATION

FIVE STEPS FOR INCREASING YOUR INFLUENCE

1. Know what you're really 'selling'.
2. Align your value with their values.
3. Demonstrate who you help them to be.
4. Develop your emotional intelligence.
5. Share your ideas, values and instructions through stories.

Team building

It turns out the soft skills are actually among the hardest to master.

In our 30 years of working with leaders and organisations around the world, we have yet to hear anyone say, 'Yeah, our people are great, it's the infrastructure and processes that give us all the trouble.'

In fact, it wouldn't be stretching the truth too far to suggest that most of the problems we face in life, both professionally and personally (and throughout history), usually find their origins in a breakdown in communication and of understanding between people (be it person to person, or collective to collective). However, even though teams and networks have this potential risk built into them by their natures, an ability to build teams and grow 'tribes', to borrow a term from Seth Godin, also offers incredible upsides and will continue to do so.

To illustrate this point, consider Gallup's Global Workforce Engagement Research. Every year, Gallup conducts a study to measure engagement in the workforce and, to be honest, the results are usually a little depressing. The most recent survey, published in 2018, pretty much reflects the results gathered in the previous years. Workforce disengagement sits where it has for a number of years, at around 50 per cent, with *active* disengagement (those who are actually white-anting the work of the rest of the organisation) making up an additional 20 per cent.

So, it turns out approximately 70 per cent either don't like the work they fill their time with, or in fact hate it.

Not great! But here's the upside: the other interesting thing that this annual report reveals is that organisations that do have an engaged workforce and a culture of collaboration and cooperation are more productive, more profitable and even have customer satisfaction ratings that sit significantly above the norm.

In other words, when your people are working well together, other things comes together also. Good news, right?

Our capacity to build teams, to work in groups, to enlist the help of others and inspire the other members of our organisations is a skill that encompasses many important behaviours: collaboration, the sharing of ideas and managing how these activities play out while allowing others to contribute and shape the work we are engaged in. So while a lot of this activity is quite serious and is applied to significant business and social undertakings, it also sounds quite a lot like play.

Dr Jason Fox, author of *The Game Changer*, often talks about why games and gamification are actually serious business. 'Games,' Fox regularly shares with his readers and audiences, 'are simply work that has been well designed.'

And the truth is, this game-like activity — forming teams, assigning roles and coordinating with others — shows up in our collective histories and throughout our lives, from our earliest childhood interactions to the very grown-up functions of management and leadership.

CRITICAL FACTORS MAKING TEAM BUILDING A FOREVER SKILL:

- ## Increasing complexity and the need for specialisation.
- ## The myth of solo success.
- ## None of us is as smart as all of us.

The nature of the work we perform has become more complicated and multifaceted. So too has the need for us to specialise in terms of expertise and to collaborate with others who are also experts in their fields.

Underscoring all this is Kenneth Blanchard's observation, the much-repeated maxim, 'None of us is as smart as all of us.'

Despite the Western world's tendency to celebrate the idea of the lone hero or the 'self-made entrepreneur', none of us actually can do much of anything alone. We all benefit from infrastructure (such as transport, communications and connectivity) that others have built for us. We use common legal frameworks and trade agreements that protect our IP, employees and trademarks. And we all operate within communities and with colleagues who support us, buy from us, advocate for us and engage with us.

Put simply, solo success has always been a myth. Teamwork is the truth.

You can better coordinate with others, drive teamwork and collaboration and build cultures of shared goals and cooperation if you:

1. Create a culture worth belonging to.
2. Break down the silos.
3. Diversify your team (and your inputs).
4. Build a 'complete' network.
5. Connect them to each other (not just to you).

1 CREATE A CULTURE WORTH BELONGING TO

We've had many conversations with Cultures at Work CEO Michael Henderson over the years. Michael is a New Zealand–based expert in culture and a corporate anthropologist with over 25 years' experience in observing, advising and educating organisations on how to enhance their workplace culture for greater levels of performance, staff fulfilment and customer delight.

He is often heard uttering gems of wisdom such as 'You can't outperform your culture'.

Cultures, of course, are not always positive, nor do they always generate the kinds of results we'd like. This is ultimately because culture is a function of our values and how those values are translated into behaviours. 'Values direct our attention and give us energy,' Michael explained. 'They're also the filter we use to evaluate those around us.'

So when we wanted to understand the role that culture plays in coordinating and informing how we work together, lift as a team and manage the performance and engagement of our people, Michael was the first person we thought of.

In his 2012 book *Chiefing Your Tribe*, Michael articulates the distinctions and interconnectedness between three important factors that build a culture — Coordination, Cooperation and Collaboration.

Michael makes the following distinctions between the three:

1. *Coordination* is a very pragmatic function that is all about working with 'hands'. It's about ensuring the right contact is made between the right data and the right people at the right time.

2. *Cooperation* is more about using the 'head' and requires greater consideration of the people and individuals involved rather than simply being outcome focused.

3. *Collaboration* is focused more on 'heart' and how the culture is functioning as an organism. Does the work enrich the community while engaging everyone involved? Is the work both rewarding socially and enjoyable personally?

So how do these three factors pull together to build culture?

Michael shared the story of the Maori tribes of New Zealand who refer to their leaders as *Rangatira*, which translates as 'weaver of people'. It's a vivid visual metaphor that evokes the idea of culture as a fabric.

According to Michael, for the Maori, 'It's more about *centreship* than leadership.' He explained that Maori leaders must be willing to be among their people, identifying as one of them, and that culture begins at the centre and radiates out, as opposed to being something that is generated in a top-down, hierarchical way.

Michael advised that a collaborative culture is one that is informed by 'Leaders worth following, performing work that is worth doing, in a culture worth belonging to, developing knowledge worth sharing.'

So how do we ensure that our cultures stay connected and that ideas and information can be shared freely and openly?

2 BREAK DOWN THE SILOS

'Break down the silos' has become a clichéd catch-cry in the corporate world, evoking images of open-plan offices, brainstorming sessions and walls decorated with innovative new ideas arranged on colourful Post-it notes. Images that, let's be honest, provoke more than a little cynicism.

However, this notion of silos is actually quite shallow and a little limiting as it encourages us to think of silos as *things* rather than as *mindsets*. In fact silos are not necessarily physical at all. We create artificial partitions and barriers between information, between roles and responsibilities, and create departments of expertise that actually reduce our capacity to communicate internally and diminish the chances of 'happy collisions' of ideas.

We sat down with Trent Innes, managing director of Xero for Asia and Australia, to discuss how we best manage our people and increase connectivity, the sharing of ideas and information, and collaborative teamwork.

His initial observation was entirely customer focused: 'Customers don't think in terms of silos or departments — neither should we.' He added, 'We're a diverse workforce serving diverse customers.'

In other words, while these silos of activity might make sense to us on a business plan or organisational flow chart, they don't necessarily reflect how we experience teams on the inside and how customers, clients and communities experience organisations from the outside.

Trent went on to explain that silos also create dysfunction between team members and barriers to serving customers. 'Breaking down those silos is critical to us getting to a shared goal more quickly.'

So, silos are bad ... but what do we do about it?

Trent suggested that in the war against silos and factions developing in an organisation, 'Empathy is critical'.

In other words, in order to reduce or eliminate siloing behaviour, we must first change our reference points for 'us' and 'them'. The more we're complaining about 'those people in accounts' or 'the compliance police', the less likely we are to see them as members of our own team and assets that help us move towards our own personal and professional goals and objectives.

This is a lesson the world of advertising learned during the Mad Men era, when one of the icons of the industry, Bill Bernbach (as well as others), decided it might be a good idea to form 'creative teams' that worked together on a *project* basis rather than having distinct functions focused on discrete *processes*. This team-building approach transformed the industry.

As the world becomes more complicated and interconnected and the problems we must solve require greater levels of creativity and interactivity, we need to build teams and organisations that facilitate greater connections and exchange, not less.

That being said, how do we ensure that the right connections are being made and that we have the right people talking to each other in a respectful and open manner?

3 DIVERSIFY YOUR TEAM (AND YOUR INPUTS)

In 2014, researchers working with MIT conducted a range of experiments to test the efficacy and benefits of workplace diversity and open collaboration. What these tests revealed, rather emphatically, was that not only is diversity a nice thing to have — it actually raises our collective IQ.

Diversity and collaboration are important in this because they help us hedge against situational or contextual blindness. In a room filled with a homogeneous group of people with similar skills, experiences and expertise, new ideas and opinions tend to be quite limited. However, access to alternative points of view and varied experiences leaves us richer, both in terms of the information we have access to and the ideas and innovation we are able to generate.

One of the great challenges of expertise is that we can become blinded by our knowledge. In other words, we know so much about the way things *have been* done, or how they *should* be done, that we can often miss how things *might* be done.

What's also important in this discussion of diversity, according to those we interviewed, is that we don't think of it as a corporate social responsibility mandate, but as a critical commercial and social asset that gives us access to points of view we might otherwise not consider.

This came up repeatedly in our research as being important at a personal, social, team and organisational level.

Neil Plumridge, managing partner for consulting at PwC, described it this way: 'You need to read outside your field of interest and seek outside input.'

The worlds of product engineering, innovation and design thinking support Neil's assertion, as we regularly find successful innovations and new thinking *inside* an industry being initiated by those who are in fact *outside* of it.

What we're really talking about here is that diversity helps us avoid a kind of 'intellectual inbreeding'. Of course, this quest for diversity of thought is often easier said than lived up to.

This is often illustrated in the world of innovation where new processes, products and services are simply adaptations from one field of endeavour to another. Ask an engineer to solve an engineering problem and you're likely to get a rather predictable engineering response. Ask a retailer, a medical professional and a user experience designer to solve the problem and the solutions presented are likely to be flavoured by the diversity of the input, giving you solutions you otherwise would not have found. Widening your inputs by broadening your team is a powerful strategy and perhaps what teamwork is truly about. We like to call this diversity of inputs 'The Avengers Principle'. Partly because we love movies and Marvel, but mostly because it reminds us that when it comes to powerful teamwork you don't want a team all with the same skills. Think about it: you don't want five Hulks. That's way too much Hulk! (Although five Captain Americas many of us could probably live with!) Yet too often that is exactly what we find.

One of the greatest challenges we find within organisational team structures is the propensity for leaders and managers to hire versions of themselves while calling it 'diversity'. It is not uncommon for a CEO to introduce us to their team and for us to meet a Chinese version of the CEO, an Indian version, a French version, a male or female version (depending on their own gender identity), and so on.

While this is one definition of diversity, we run the risk of having the same conversations, just with different accents.

Obviously diversity of ethnicity, gender and sexuality are incredibly important and we're certainly not arguing against using them as a filter for building a team that is broadly experienced and divergently robust. However what is commonly overlooked is the need for cognitive diversity: a variety of thinking and processing styles.

Frank Ribuot, CEO of global recruiting firm Randstad in Australia, indicated that the increasing complexity of the work we do makes diversity and a capacity to collaborate even more important than it has ever been.

However, he also suggested that we do this deliberately and strategically rather than simply allowing diversity to just 'show up'.

Frank suggests five questions to consider before adding someone to your team. They are useful filters to ensure you get enough diversity in your team without compromising its effectiveness and cohesiveness:

1. Do they challenge me?
2. Do they see the world differently to me?
3. Do I like them?
4. Do I trust them?
5. Can I sit on a five-hour flight next to them?

Implicit in each of Frank's questions, and in the broader conversation we had with him, is the need for respect. In other words, our mental framing for diversity needs to come from a perspective of contribution and enrichment rather than one of simply 'ticking the corporate boxes'.

In heeding Neil's and Frank's advice, how might we be more strategic in seeking diversity of people and input?

4 BUILD A 'COMPLETE' NETWORK

Given our quite natural bias to want to surround ourselves with like-minded thinkers, who then should we look to include in our teams and our personal and professional networks?

This has been an ongoing conversation over many years between us and networking and collaboration expert Janine Garner, who we mentioned earlier in chapter 4. In fact, Kieran and Janine regularly run leadership development programs for multinational corporations all around the world, and Janine is often called in as a specialist on the subject of collaboration or networking in our own leadership programs at The Impossible Institute. In other words, she's a big part of making sure our own network is 'complete'.

Without going into the full gamut of Janine's work in this field, it's worth considering her advice on four key people we need in our network as well as four personality types we might need to manage or else eliminate altogether.

If we're going to build diverse and successful teams, Garner suggests we need:

- *Promoters.* Promoters are the people who cheerlead our successes, who are always in our corners and advocating for our dreams and potential. They want us to *become more.*

- *Pit Crew.* Our pit crew are those who sustain us, 'repair us' and keep us going when times get tough. They help us build a sense of resilience and help us keep our emotions from overwhelming us. They want us to *care more.*

- *Teachers.* Teachers help us to increase our knowledge and awareness. They may have already achieved what we want to and act as mentors or they might simply challenge our thinking and understanding around an issue. They want us to *know more.*

- *Butt Kickers.* We all know these people and yet they are often under-appreciated. They usually know us well, *too well,* in fact, and they're unlikely to buy into our BS or let us get away with it. They want us to *do more.*

Garner also suggests there are those we might consciously want to exclude from our network and team:

- *Burners.* Burners like to keep you small, to fill your head with doubts and encourage you to stay within the lines and play to the status quo. They want you to *be less.*

- *Underminers.* Got a stabbing feeling between your shoulder blades? That's how Underminers make you feel. They're nice to your face but make you feel like you constantly need to defend and justify yourself. They want us to *care less.*

- *Judgers.* Of course, good judgement is a great thing, however it can become toxic when it breeds negativity or limits your potential and stifles growth. They want us to *know less.*

- *Fighters.* These people are just hard work. They are the people you feel like you have to wrestle in the direction of success on a daily basis. They don't challenge you out of rigour or improvement but out of pure bloody-mindedness. They want us to *do less.*

Clearly, we need a range of different thinking and abilities in our networks and our teams, but the truth is, none of us are mono-talented. In fact, our outside and personal interests, things that often sit quite apart from our job descriptions, are often incredibly useful and allow us a broader perspective and insight, even within our own thinking.

One final thought on the need for a complete team or network: *Focus on results, not just roles.* In other words, don't limit a team member's capacity to contribute by their job title or their role description. We need more people to bring all of themselves to every part of their lives. We always will.

5 CONNECT THEM TO EACH OTHER (NOT JUST TO YOU)

When you have a relationship with a member of your team, you have only a single connection and therefore one point of failure with no backup. When an entire team is interconnected and derives social and personal reward and status from being a part of the network, there are multiple connections. This means no single point of failure is catastrophic.

This is the mistake many leaders who model their leadership style on the 'charismatic hero' fall into.

Obviously, there's something very seductive about thinking of yourself as the inspirational leader that everyone looks to. The ego thinks to itself, 'Before I inspired them with my noble *why*, their lives were bereft of meaning!!!' It makes us walk a little taller with a little more swagger. However, it also has within it a fatal flaw — *us*!

A far better strategy, in the pursuit of building effective teams, is the idea of building interconnected networks that are more 'web-like' and less 'tower-like'.

The more individuals see themselves as part of something bigger, as contributing to a broader picture, the more likely they are to think of themselves as irrevocably connected.

This requires all of the facets of team building we've just examined: an ability to create the basis for a culture worth belonging to where ideas and information are freely exchanged between diverse teams of varied experiences and expertise. Most importantly, it requires the capacity to create an environment where people feel not just connected to the leader, or even to the cause, but to each other as well.

∞

Teams have changed history, brought down and built empires. They have driven the human race forward. The need for working in teams, building teams and leveraging the power of the collective will not diminish. Rather it is likely to increase. This means your ability to work well in, connect with, lead and inspire teams is eternal.

APPLICATION

FIVE STEPS FOR BETTER TEAM BUILDING

1. Create a culture worth belonging to.
2. Break down the silos.
3. Diversify your team (and your inputs).
4. Build a 'complete' network.
5. Connect them to each other (not just to you).

Trust

Your reputation is not what you say about yourself. It is what other people say when you're not in the room.

In a *New York Times* interview published in April of 2016, Tobias Lütke, CEO of Shopify, describes a metaphor they use within the organisation to measure the level of trust that exists between team members. They call it a 'trust battery'.

It represents something that we're all familiar with but we may not always be consciously aware of or know how to describe or create: *trust*.

Tobias outlines the process like this: When you start work at the organisation your trust battery has a 50 per cent charge. Then, over time, the battery either gains or loses charge based on the interactions you have with other team members. Have you lived up to your word and worked efficiently and harmoniously with other members of the team?

Essentially, it gives the Shopify team a shared language and visual metaphor that allows them to discuss what human beings do intuitively in a highly practical and easily relatable way.

It's a modern expression of a skill that has always been important. Trust solidifies our personal relationships, drives sales in our businesses and elevates our standing in our communities.

Ultimately, trust is informed by and maintains our reputation. Are we a trusted authority in our field? Someone who is count-on-able in our team? Are we the 'go to' expert others rely on when push comes to shove?

Trust is also a rather fragile thing, slow to earn and quick to lose. An old Dutch saying posits that 'Trust arrives walking and leaves riding'. Part of what makes trust so tenuous, and possibly fleeting, is that trust and reputation are largely linked to the opinions of other people. For example, if you tell us you're good at something, that's one thing. But if someone whose opinion we already trust tells us you're good, that is quite another thing.

In other words, a capacity to generate trust requires an ability to not only communicate your usefulness and expertise with others, but a capacity to demonstrate that you can walk the talk also.

As the American philosopher Ralph Waldo Emerson once quipped, 'What you do speaks so loudly I cannot hear what you are saying.'

CRITICAL FACTORS MAKING TRUST A FOREVER SKILL:

- **Accountability is increasing as people have greater and more immediate access to information.**
- **We're more connected which means opinions can now be amplified more quickly and more widely.**
- **Trust beats truth (a fact that makes many of us very uneasy).**

As connectivity increases and individuals are able to generate the kind of attention and authority that used to only be available to huge corporations with deep pockets, trust will only grow in importance.

This connectivity allows our opinions and observations to be shared, reviewed and amplified with increasing speed. It also allows the Davids of the world to hold the Goliaths to account. Customers with a grievance used to call a complaints centre and have a private conversation with a staff member of a large multinational. Today, they tweet their annoyances and we get to watch and judge how the corporation responds in a very public arena.

Throughout the interviews and research we conducted, trust was identified as the ultimate intangible asset. For that reason, we've deemed it a Forever Skill.

You can build trust if you:

1. Develop some thought leadership.
2. Nurture your community.
3. Tell the truth with vulnerability.
4. Practise 'story-doing'.
5. Make your ideas 'pass-on-able'.

1 DEVELOP SOME THOUGHT LEADERSHIP

'Thought leadership' has become one of those hot corporate terms that is probably overused and not particularly well understood.

For our purposes, we define thought leadership as a high degree of expertise or competency narrowly focused on a particular field or skill set. In other words, it is the thing that people come to you for because they know that you're the best in the biz.

We discussed this concept over many cups of coffee, glasses of wine and courses of lunch and dinner with Matt Church, the founder and chair of Thought Leaders Global. (Just to be clear, this was not over the course of one sitting.)

Matt's definition of thought leadership adds some important context to our own.

He suggests that thought leadership goes beyond mere expertise and that it in fact requires an ability to create new and distinct intellectual property that adds to the canon of existing knowledge and wisdom in your professional sphere.

In other words, it's a capacity to move your field of endeavour forward. To advance and augment rather than to simply understand and retell.

We think this is a pretty important distinction to make, as there are many experts in the world who are highly competent in their jobs or roles but have yet to contribute or add anything new to their craft. It's important to note here that Matt believes these experts still play a critical role in lifting the shared understanding of the collective wisdom that already exists. Many teachers, for example, demonstrate just how incredibly important this function is, whether they have added to the intellectual property of the field or not.

However, to be a thought leader, in Matt's estimation, an expert who is not only seen as competent but a trusted authority in their field, you must also add to the work of those who have gone before you. In other words, as the Isaac Newton quote we mentioned in our acknowledgements so eloquently phrased it, see further by 'standing on the shoulders of the giants' who have preceded you.

History books have noted many thought leaders who did just this (and we are certain the books have missed a great many more). They will continue to do so whether they come in the form of books or plug-ins for our minds. Thought leaders move us forward. Often they challenge us, our ways of thinking, our ways of doing things and the comfort of the status quo. This means we will always need them if we want progress.

This capacity of a thought leader, to not only understand your professional or social realm, but to improve it, adds to your authority and increases the trust others have for your work in it. Learning some of the skills thought leadership requires would be a wise investment.

2 NURTURE YOUR COMMUNITY

You don't need to be famous or a celebrity to garner trust; you simply need to be the person your community, your company or peers turn to when they need expertise, an empathetic ear or a sense of certainty.

This capacity to nurture community was immediately apparent when we interviewed French restaurateur David Bitton.

As a teenager, David packed his bags and left his home in Paris to enter the world of five-star hotels and fine dining, a journey that would take him around the world and into some of the most illustrious kitchens on the planet.

One lesson he learned very early on from one of his mentors was to get out of the kitchen and talk to the diners he was serving; to get to know and understand them and what they cared about. This lesson has perhaps been more determinant of David's success than any recipe or cooking technique he learned along the way. In time, he learned that he needed to allow his customers to 'meet the human being behind the business', and, in doing so, build a community of trust and engagement.

His current business, a chic little café rather aptly named Bitton, is built on that same philosophy. He is almost always to be found walking the floor engaging with customers, many of whom have been regulars for almost 20 years, and continuing conversations that they had begun in previous weeks ... and sometimes, previous years!

Using an expression that only a Frenchman could get away with, he explained, 'I want my staff to make love to everyone who walks in.' His goal is to create a space that is familiar, safe and a home away from home.

However, the connections that David has built are not simply between himself or his staff and their diners, they have also been built between the regulars. Sipping a coffee at Bitton and watching the regulars come and go is akin to watching an episode of the US sitcom *Cheers*. You almost expect the arrival of a portly local to prompt the greeting, 'Hey Norm!'

Of course, David has generated his own celebrity over the years and regularly appears on television shows as a guest celebrity chef. But this is not why people come to Bitton. They come to be seen, to be recognised and to feel special. David has created a space where his diners feel a sense of safety, connectedness and trust.

Unlike most restaurants and cafés that serve their local communities, such as those within walking distance or the passing trade on the drive between home and work, Bitton has become a 'destination' café. In other words, the community that David has built is so strong, so compelling and so desirable that people are willing to travel significant distances in order to feel a part of it.

The community and reputation David Bitton has built is the core of his business and his commercial success. 'Sure, the food is good and the coffee is good, but that's not why people come to Bitton,' he explained (although clearly this admission is a difficult one for a formally trained French chef).

In the end, they come for the community and because they know that they are going to be welcomed, to enjoy a communal experience and because they trust those who serve them to make them feel welcome and accepted. The need this satisfies is not going away anytime soon, if ever.

3 TELL THE TRUTH WITH VULNERABILITY

When you work in the worlds of marketing, advertising and branding, it is hardly unusual to find people exaggerating the positives and playing down any negatives. However, what we've found throughout our careers, and in the research for this book, is that those who are willing to own their 'inconvenient truth' (to borrow a phrase from former US vice president Al Gore), those who make themselves vulnerable and more human, are the ones who elicit the most trust.

When we interviewed our good friend and business celebrity Jeffrey Hayzlett, it was hard to ignore the power of his identity.

Jeffrey is a former C-suite executive of a Fortune 500 US company, was a celebrity business adviser on US President Donald Trump's *The Apprentice* and is the founder and chief executive of the C-Suite Network, a media and advisory organisation that helps C-suite executives stay at the top of their game.

Jeffrey's presence and identity is immediate. He's a South Dakota boy who made it big in the Big Apple. He's big, direct and expressive, and whenever we meet with him he's dressed in a blazer with a flashy and colourful lining and wearing cowboy boots beneath his jeans. He describes himself as a 'business cowboy'.

Now, rather than hiding his regional roots, Jeffrey has turned this identity into an asset. He's conscious that in many parts of the world, Americans can receive ... let's call them 'mixed reviews'. But rather than shying away from that, he amplifies it.

When he's outside of the United States, Jeffrey will walk on stage and say, 'I know some of you are thinking: "Great! Another loud, opinionated American!" Well … *I am not going to disappoint you!'*

In other words, Jeffrey has turned what might be a weakness into an asset.

Of course, a capacity to be unexpectedly honest can also build trust during moments of crisis.

Some years ago, we were lucky enough to share the stage with Richard Champion de Crespigny in Bangkok, Thailand.

Richard was the pilot in command of flight QF32, an A380 that was en route from London to Sydney via Singapore when an uncontained engine failure created enormous holes in the wing (something all aeronautical experts agree is not an ideal situation).

The speech Richard gave in Bangkok was the first time he had shared his story publicly. What was fascinating was the fact that his response to the crisis has now influenced Qantas's crisis strategy and is being adopted all around the world.

When we sat down with Richard after his speech, what we were most interested in was how his strategy was distinct to that of other pilots at the time. The key distinction seemed to be Richard's capacity to 'overshare'. He stayed in constant contact with the passengers, sharing updates more often and more openly than had been the norm. The result? A plane filled with calm passengers despite what they could all see was happening outside their windows.

Confusion, uncertainty and helplessness induce fear and dread when we are unsure of our situation. These fears escalate when no one takes responsibility, is in control or is contactable. Fears turn into panic that spreads rapidly when our emotional and logical minds feed-back and reinforce each other. These emotions are often more frightening than the problem itself. The key during a crisis is to communicate you are in control, actively dealing with the issue and then un-powering people's fears. Tell the truth, explain what has happened, what will happen and what every person must do. And when you think you have communicated enough, double it. When you resolve people's fears and give them a path to safety, that is when you create calm, teamwork and trust.

There was no point denying the Airbus was in trouble. What did make sense was contextualising it in a way that set passengers' fears at ease and reinforced their trust in the leader. Disclosing the truth, humility and personal vulnerability makes human beings more trusting. Perhaps it should come as no surprise, as the underlying logic makes complete sense. If you are honest about something negative, people will believe you and respond with trust and support.

So how does vulnerability feed the expectation of truthfulness and build trust? What's critical to understand here is that, by being vulnerable, humble, exposed, we create the impression that we are open and transparent. By humbling ourselves rather than talking ourselves up, we establish an impression of having nothing to hide — this impression very often converts to trust and to engagement.

This phenomenon reminded us of one of the most extraordinary organisations from the land of the long white cloud, Aotearoa. The New Zealand All Blacks have dominated the global rugby world for decades, despite coming from a country with the national population of a mid-size city.

Despite this, in an article published by *News Hub Sports,* the All Blacks reportedly have a 77 per cent winning percentage, a result that is almost unheard of in professional sports.

Their superpower? An ethos of vulnerability and humility.

They have a culture built around the idea that no individual is more important than the team, or the team's ancestors. This shows up in their practice of 'sweeping the sheds'.

David Knies in his book *Breaking Away* explains that they all sweep the sheds after the game. 'Everyone is responsible for the smallest details — including cleaning out the locker room after training or a match. Sweeping the shed is your job, no matter who you are.'

Now, is this what we usually imagine when we think of world-class athletes? Or do we picture media images of lives of excess and hyper-inflated egos?

The All Blacks trust their legacy, their rituals, their teammates and leaders.

By being vulnerable, humble and transparent, the All Blacks have built a community and culture of openness. No-one feels the need to talk themselves up and trust ensues.

Trust is powerful; it always has been.

4 PRACTISE 'STORY-DOING'

'Story-doing' is the embodiment of the Ralph Waldo Emerson quote we mentioned earlier. It might also be paraphrased as, 'When you walk your talk, others talk about it too'.

This thinking was echoed throughout our interview with Shep Hyken.

Shep is one of the most influential customer service experts in the United States and around the world. His best-selling book, *The Amazement Revolution*, is a testament to delivering above and beyond customers' expectations.

We sat down with Shep to talk to him about why he thinks an ability to build a 'behaviour-based reputation' is critical to building a personal brand, establishing authority in your industry and community, as well as generating positive word of mouth.

Shep's guiding ethos is that people do business with people, not organisations, even in the online space. 'This is an awesome responsibility,' Shep added. 'You get to make the difference' and to have an impact regardless of your role within the organisation.'

This is critical, in Shep's opinion. The reputation of an airline, for example, is vulnerable at every touchpoint. The flight might be on time, the food pleasant and the in-flight service exceptional, but if my checked baggage arrives dented or torn, that one experience damages the entire airline's reputation.

Conversely, when something amazing happens, something we weren't expecting, something surprising and exciting, we tell that story to everyone we meet.

This is the essence of story-doing, a capacity to do something so extraordinary that people can't help but share the story with others.

This is as relevant to individuals and leaders building their personal and professional reputations as it is to large organisations creating powerful brands. We've all experienced broken promises and unmet expectations in both of these contexts, but likewise, we've all probably experienced the opposite, where our expectations were not only met, but exceeded to such a degree that we just had to share the story.

The restaurant staff member who remembers our name, our birthday or our favourite table; the retailer who displays an uncommon awareness or empathy for those they serve; and the leader who takes the time not only to help us raise our performance but to see who we are and meet us at that level. These are the experiences we share with our peers and friends. No-one tells stories of the expected — we only share and pass on the extraordinary.

Which of course leads us to point number five...

5 MAKE YOUR IDEAS 'PASS-ON-ABLE'

According to Nielsen's Global Trust in Advertising Survey conducted in 2015, 88 per cent of us now rely on friend recommendations before making any purchase decision (a figure that actually rises to over 90 per cent in many parts of the world).

Now, this reliance on friend and peer recommendations is nothing new. We're absolutely convinced that in the hills of ancient Greece, people in chitons and sandals would lean over a neighbour's fence and ask, 'I'm thinking of buying a donkey...you know a good donkey dealership?'

However, the digital revolution has amplified this behaviour in a way very few of us could ever have conceived of, even just ten years ago.

For example, Trip Advisor is arguably one of the most, if not *the* most, influential travel organisations on the planet. They don't own any hotels, fleets of aircraft, coaches or ships, and they aren't representatives of any particular nation's travel authority. All they essentially do is curate other people's opinions.

In other words, their entire business model and authority is built on trust and reputation rather than the budget and scale of a marketing campaign.

What's most interesting in this conversation around trust is that consumers, communities and constituents are no longer paying much attention to corporate advertising or political shills; they're listening to like-minded voices who now have a way to turn up the volume using technology.

Where once organisations could pay to buy a share of your attention with our communications, now we rely on 'pass-on-ability'. In fact, pass-on-ability often trumps credibility in the old-fashioned sense of the word.

We were working with nutritionists who had spent years studying food and human physiology. They were complaining how unfair it was that people trusted Instagram 'experts' more than them. Unlike the fit, tanned, scantily clad Insta experts, they had studied! But as we told them, perhaps their degree had not given them everything they needed. What they were missing is the idea of pass-on-ability. The Instagram experts built trust by making things easy to share and connect with, whereas the nutritionists kept themselves apart from the customers. Seeing a beautiful pic of a meal an Insta expert had for breakfast and getting inspired was more powerful than a conversation and a printed out list of 'do eat's and 'don't eat's.

If you want to earn trust you have to connect.

Trust is rarely conferred based on our own assessment of ourselves; it is far more linked to what others say about us and how those stories are shared across networks of trust.

∞

The capacity to generate and elicit a sense of trust is a skill that is probably as old as humanity itself. However, its importance and applications are not only increasing, they are accelerating.

Trust requires an ability to develop some thought leadership, to become proficient and expert in some field or endeavour, to nurture a community around this service, to amplify our trustworthiness through transparency, vulnerability and by walking our talk. All of which helps others to pass on their experiences with us to others, to build trust on our behalf and help our reputations to precede us into every room we walk into.

Your ability to build trust and be trusted will always set you in good stead for success.

FIVE STEPS FOR BUILDING TRUST

1. Develop some thought leadership.
2. Nurture your community.
3. Tell the truth with vulnerability.
4. Practise 'story-doing'.
5. Make your ideas 'pass-on-able'.

Translation

**Communication isn't about the
transmission and reception of information;
it's about moving towards a shared sense
of meaning.**

One of the most critical breakage points in human communication lies in the difference between what is said, written or visualised and what is understood. In fact, most of the challenges we faced in researching this book stemmed from this fact.

Seemingly self-explanatory words such as 'leadership', 'creativity' and 'resilience' mean quite different things to different people. In fact, in different circumstances, the same sets of words, phrases, tones of voice and imagery can simultaneously evoke passion, inspiration, offence and even rage.

We all intuitively understand this, and yet most of our communication strategies are based on communication models that do not take this into account. These models teach us to think in terms of transmission and reception (filtered through interference), when human communication is far more nuanced and much less linear.

For this reason, translation — a capacity to assess, curate, interpret and share ideas and information across different professional, social and cultural spheres — is a Forever Skill.

CRITICAL FACTORS MAKING TRANSLATION A FOREVER SKILL:

- **We're overloaded with information.**
- **Understanding is more important than accuracy.**
- **Teaching, instruction and mentoring are 'forever needs'.**

One of the fallacies we've bought into around human communication is the drive to deliver messages that are both complete and accurate, when, in fact, neither are particularly necessary to create a shared sense of understanding. Indeed, too much detail can lead to comprehension decay.

Consider the abbreviated phrases we all rely on in everyday conversation or our use of simple body language and facial expressions that convey as much meaning, and a great deal more emotion, than any academic white paper.

Conversely, the same factors can have precisely the opposite effect. Visual cues and simplified slang can often be misinterpreted if we are not completely conscious of how they are being received or the context in which we are using them.

For example, one of the authors, let's call him 'Dan', is often interviewed on television about business strategy and social trends. During one such panel interview, Dan was sitting next to a long-time professional peer and good friend and listening intently to what she had to say.

After the interview, Dan received a call from his sister who remarked, 'Wow, you really hate her!' After explaining that the woman was, in fact, a very good friend, his sister replied, 'Then you really need to work on your RBF' (Resting Bitch Face). There are some truths only a sibling can share with you.

The point is, what was being communicated was the complete opposite of what was intended and being experienced on *Dan's side* of the conversation. Intense interest was being read as contempt.

This scenario plays out in just about every area of human interaction, from our personal relationships (think John Gray's *Men Are from Mars and Women Are from Venus*) to interactions between professionals working in separate silos and from different technical backgrounds, to the interactions we have with customers and our community.

Add a little pressure or stress to these situations and the risk of being misunderstood intensifies.

So how can we all improve our capacity to adapt our communication to different circumstances, applications and audiences without all of us receiving a call from Dan's sister?

1. Simplify the complex.
2. Curate the information that matters.
3. Use the appropriate language.
4. Think in terms of education, not information distribution.
5. Make your ideas accessible, achievable and actionable.

1 SIMPLIFY THE COMPLEX

We welcome feedback after delivering a speech or training workshop. But if there is one piece of feedback that causes us to see the red mist, it is this: 'You need to dumb it down. Our people aren't that smart.'

While this is incredibly insulting to and judgemental of the team they're referring to, as with most things, there is a lesson hidden inside the insult. Rather than 'dumbing things down', the real opportunity lies in simplifying the complex.

As Albert Einstein is famously quoted as saying, 'If you can't explain it simply, you don't understand it well enough.' (But then, what would he know?)

Simplification has been an important tool of translation throughout history. However, as our attention spans and cognitive bandwidth shrink to 30-second videos, love notes in the form of emojis, and 140 to 280–character tweets, its importance isn't in any danger of diminishing.

So what techniques can we enlist to help us simplify an ever more complicated world?

- *Metaphor.* Metaphor and comparison are perhaps the simplest form of translation there is — linking the new to what is already familiar and understood.

- *Brevity.* This is a capacity to eliminate the unnecessary. Try writing what you want to say in longhand, and then remove words until it no longer makes sense. Then replace the last word you removed.

- *Chunking down.* It's said that 'the best way to eat an elephant is one bit at a time'. (Best read as a metaphor, not a serving suggestion.) This ability to chunk a process down into achievable steps and to communicate these steps to our teams is also essential in tackling any complicated task or undertaking.

- *Easy wins.* An important way to build engagement and confidence is to create easy wins and build on that progress. This line of thinking should be used to prioritise the steps used in chunking down the process.

- *Identify essentials.* Most of the time, success doesn't depend upon us having all of the information at the same time, or even before we begin. What this means is, we need to prioritise what is essential, what can wait and what can be ignored altogether. In other words, we need to learn to curate.

2 CURATE THE INFORMATION THAT MATTERS

Over 800 years ago, the Persian poet Rumi said, 'The art of knowing is knowing what to ignore.'

Rarely has ancient wisdom seemed more applicable to the modern world. Today, we don't suffer from a lack of information — in fact, we are all overloaded.

Translation isn't simply the interpretation or redeployment of information, it is also an ability to understand what is necessary and poignant, and just as importantly, what is not.

Professionals such as Irish productivity expert Dermot Crowley now spend a large proportion of their consulting time helping leaders, professionals and organisations manage their increasingly over-burdened inboxes.

All of which is hardly surprising. We no longer measure data in bits and bytes but in zetabytes and exabytes, metrics that use metaphoric comparisons to *the number of grains of sand on the planet* to create a relative sense of scale.

Complicating this even further is the fact that the number of information sources vying for our attention has also increased, and we are spectacularly under-resourced when it comes to checking the credibility of these sources.

Add to that internet biases and social media filter bubbles (the tendency for the internet to feed our own opinions back to us), and you have a potent risk of misinformation, misunderstanding and missed opportunities.

This is a theme we picked up on when we sat down to have a coffee and a chat with the CEO of Pittard Training, Gary Pittard. Gary's specialty is helping professionals in the real estate industry build profitable and scalable businesses, but today, served up with our java, we also got a slice of wisdom as to why we need to curate the information we communicate.

Gary's advice was to first 'Understand what a win looks like and to decide what is essential in achieving that win'.

As an avid lifelong learner, Gary also shared that there were so many fields of study and skills we could be applying our minds to, but before we do that it is essential that we ask the question: 'What should I be studying right now?'

He added that while it was critical for us to curate the information we should be paying attention to, it was equally important to decide the information that needed to be curated *out* of our field of attention.

He explained that too often we continue with behaviours and strategies that no longer make sense, partly out of habit and legacy, but also because we rarely take stock and audit our information resources and our own communication patterns to assess what is no longer necessary or even counterproductive.

Ultimately, curation of information is an exercise in prioritisation. It is the ability to focus on what truly matters and to not be distracted by the things that do not ... or at least, those that do not matter yet.

3 USE THE APPROPRIATE LANGUAGE

It has been frequently observed that English-speaking foreign tourists, when failing to be understood by the locals, decide to double down and say exactly the same thing, only LOUDER!

It's a cliché, but like many clichés, it's true enough to be worth repeating.

This anecdote matters because we all demonstrate this kind of behaviour in many aspects of our lives. It affects our communication across generations, whether it's from parent to child or child to parent. It clouds communication between senior executives and the teams in their charge. It also plays out in cross-cultural conversations: between different industry sectors, ethnicities, communities and from one communications tool to another, for example from verbal to visual to audiovisual or the written word.

Where we can run into trouble in this regard is that we all tend to have an inherent bias and preference towards one or two modes of communication. These biases, of course, may not align quite so neatly with those we are looking to engage with.

Before launching into a conversation, a presentation, a pitch or even a marketing campaign, it's worth considering whether we're filtering through our own language biases or those of our audience.

Clearly, there are many different 'languages' we can enlist in communication:

- visual
- technical
- professional
- cultural
- situational.

(And the list of languages available to us is decidedly longer than what we have just outlined.)

An appropriate example of how this plays out is the story of the London Tube Map.

Like most major cities around the world, London has an expansive underground train network connecting commuters from one side of the city to the other.

For locals, navigating the Tube has become instinctive and intuitive. But this wasn't always the case.

In an effort to help London commuters find their way around the Tube, the London Transport Authority decided upon a rather obvious course of action: get some cartographers and create a map.

However, despite the bullet-proof logic of this approach and the expertise of the people they charged with the task, they ended up creating maps that were far too detailed and impossible for anyone other than a cartographer to interpret.

In other words, there was too much information, and it was communicated using the wrong language.

In the end, the Tube map that was adopted, which has become the convention for underground railway maps the world over, was created by someone who had no experience in map-making and could therefore ignore relative distance and scale.

Interestingly, neither had he even been hired to do the job! The concept was created by an electrical technician named Henry Charles Beck in his spare time. As someone used to looking at electrical schematics that were informative precisely because they were simplified and even dimensionally inaccurate, he was well placed to create the map.

What this teaches us is that a capacity to translate your ideas, information and vision into the appropriate communications channel and language is critical.

However, this is more than just a question of language — it's also a function of tonality and expression.

We spoke to MD and resilience expert Dan Diamond in his home in Bremerton, Washington, in the Pacific Northwest of the United States. We talked about the importance of humour as a tool to drive perspective and open-mindedness.

Dan is not alone in making this observation about humour. Edward de Bono, the father of lateral thinking, once described humour as the highest level of abstract thinking.

Dan shared with us that humour is an incredibly important tool of translation as it allows us to develop greater peripheral vision and also to cope under stress. While humour may not immediately appear to be an appropriate choice of language for the medical fraternity, its appropriateness is very much determined by context and intent.

He explained to us that humour is incredibly important, and in serious professional pursuits such as medicine, perhaps even more so. 'It's a way to relieve pressure,' he continued, 'to step out of the rapids and sit on the bank for a while.'

The language of humour helps us to maintain our humanity in the face of tragedy and to broaden our points of view. Tragedy is not made any more significant by our seriousness but might be rendered more bearable through the lens of humour.

The choice and use of the appropriate language for the context we are in and the audience we are looking to engage is a critical function of translation.

4 THINK IN TERMS OF EDUCATION NOT INFORMATION DISTRIBUTION

School principals are almost always a little intimidating. As much as we'd like to think this is a vestige of the relative size difference we experience as young children, when we meet up with former school principal Adam Voigt, we realise this is simply wishful thinking.

Adam stands at about 193 centimetres (6 feet 4 inches) tall and is built like a rugby player. In the nicest possible way, Adam is a *big unit* of a man! What's surprising, however, is that he has the demeanour and countenance of a gentle giant. Former students may, of course, choose to disagree with our assessment.

Today Adam works as an education expert and a consultant who helps organisations build learning cultures, so we wanted to get his take on the value of education in the Forever Skill of translation.

'Years ago, education was seen as a distribution model,' he observed, 'but the internet broke that. Information is now ubiquitous.' Of course, as Adam explained, the ubiquity of information doesn't necessarily lead to greater education or understanding.

Today we're too busy trying to cram information in when we should be allowing for experimentation. Today, there's almost no trial and error. There's no space to be wrong and to learn from that. 'Learn' is supposed to be a verb.

So what skills does Adam consider critical to helping us translate ideas and information into education?

He started off by framing his belief that 'Information isn't enough. "Right" isn't enough.' Education requires a capacity to work with multiple tools, languages and tonalities to help learners anchor what they are being taught in a very practical way. He suggested that we should:

- *Focus on progress.* Rather than being caught up in perfectionism we should make improvement the goal.

- *Make that progress visible.* The best educators are both firm and fair, not one or the other. This means having a capacity to translate feedback into a format that inspires rather than cripples.

- *Be entertaining in the way we deliver information.* Learning should be memorable and interesting.

- *Empathise with those we're instructing.* 'This goes beyond sympathy. It's about understanding how what you're teaching impacts those you are training.'

- *Learn to assess the correct problems.* 'We need to discriminate and assess what's really important, to manage cognitive load and decide what is actually bullshit.'

Ultimately, education is one of the most important applications of translation as, by its very nature, it is not just about the transmission of information but rather, as Adam suggests, it is about using that information to raise understanding and increase competence.

This leads us to our next observation about translation.

5 MAKE YOUR IDEAS ACCESSIBLE, ACHIEVABLE AND ACTIONABLE

When we first met Holly Ransom a decade ago, she was a 19-year-old with prodigious potential. A fact that made her admirable and deeply annoying in equal measure!

Her potential and intelligence were immediately apparent, and she is very much living up to them as CEO of consulting firm Emergent, as the co-chair on the United Nations Youth G20 Summit, as a board member for the Port Adelaide AFL club and as an expert who helps organisations engage and get the most out of their next-generation talent.

We spoke to Holly about the need to build confidence in those we work with by building on achievable wins and creating a bias to success. This requires an ability to translate intent and instructions into practicality and actions.

She talked to us about the need to translate our *whats* and *whys* into *hows*. '*How* matters as much as *what* and *why*,' she advised us. 'We need to give our people some positive action they can take as a result of what we've shared with them.'

It's a thought that was echoed by Jason Forrest, the CEO and chief culture officer of FPG in Fort Worth, Texas. Jason is an award-winning leadership and sales coach who is an expert at creating high-performance, high-profit, and 'Best Place to Work' cultures.

Jason suggested, 'We need to break things down for people, make things bite-sized, digestible and executable.' He advocated for seeing our role as leaders from the perspective of 'producing other leaders'.

'Ultimately,' he shared, 'we're in the business of making other people smarter.'

What this all means for us in developing the Forever Skill of translation is that we need to shift our focus from that of broadcasting *information out* to one of lifting *understanding up*. Translation, therefore, might be thought of as shifting from the context of source information, or from our own points of view, to helping those we are communicating with to experience our intended meaning.

∞

Whether it's person to person, person to people, people to people or even person to machine in the future some time, translation is a skill that is crucial. Being able to say something in such a way that someone else can not just hear it, but act on it, has always been powerful. It always will be.

APPLICATION

FIVE STEPS FOR BECOMING BETTER AT TRANSLATION

1. Simplify the complex.
2. Curate the information that matters.
3. Use the appropriate language.
4. Think in terms of education not information distribution.
5. Make your ideas accessible, achievable and actionable.

PART

3

CONTROL SKILLS

'NO MAN IS FIT TO COMMAND ANOTHER,
THAT CANNOT COMMAND HIMSELF.'

William Penn

The last of our Forever Skills clusters is *Control*.

In some ways, this might be considered the most problematic of the three clusters of Forever Skills, as the very concept of control has rather a lot of baggage associated with it. You may even be feeling a little uncomfortable right now and less than excited to read on.

Depending on your political or philosophical views, the word 'control' might conjure up authoritarian or militaristic imagery, planned economic systems and government overreach and bureaucracy. Alternatively, one might consider control to be contrary to natural law or an unfair impingement on our spirituality.

The truth is, we often think of control as being the antithesis of freedom of any kind. This is possibly because our initial experience of control is that of being a child with very little, surrounded by adults who seem to have more than we would like. Commands such as 'Go to bed', 'Eat your broccoli', and 'Share your toys', are hardly likely to leave us appreciating control, given that it appears to only be directed towards us.

However, despite this discomfort with the word 'control', what emerged from our research is that an ability to understand it, use it, apply it and negotiate with it is a critical consideration in terms of the skills that the future will demand.

Perhaps it is useful at this stage to broaden our definition of 'control' from one of authority that is placed over us, to one of consensus around where power and energy should be applied and just who should be able to wield it.

It's also worth considering control as it applies at a micro as well as macro level. The ability to self-regulate our behaviour is considered by most to be critical to any kind of personal, physical and financial achievement. Control is not simply something that is directed outwardly, or towards us — it is also an ability to have power over ourselves, our focus and how we react to the world.

Of course, as our social systems have grown and become more complicated, from small tribal units to civilisations of many millions, the need for control and an agreed sense of where power should lie has become increasingly important.

The need for control also applies to far more than just behaviour. It also informs how we choose to share and use resources, where our focus should be applied, what we consider to be good, correct and valuable as a society and how we spend our time and even who we spend it with.

We've identified four controls skills that are important to understand and develop:

1. self-control

2. resource management

3. order

4. implementation.

So let's have a deeper examination of the Forever Skills related to control.

Self-control

In the end, all we are really in control of is the realm of our own minds.

Imogen Quinn is an extraordinary young woman. She picked up a virus overseas when she was fourteen, and by the time she was in her final year of school, her health had deteriorated to such an extent, that at times she was non-verbal and non-mobile. She has pervasive brain fog, pain and debilitating exhaustion, and while most young people her age were cramming for exams, socialising and planning life beyond school, Imogen was requiring assistance to effectively communicate and do the most basic of tasks.

'I know I should know how to read the words, but I don't,' she told us with a calmness and acceptance that is inspiring. When we asked her what she was learning about herself she was unbelievably poised and articulate, and has a perspective few adults would demonstrate in such a challenging time. a

Her mum calls it 'grace' and Imogen has it in copious quantities. She is strong and quietly determined. She doesn't complain. She focuses on the work she is doing and the progress she is making. She is graceful about it.

Imogen teaches us all that the ability to deal with the situation you find yourself in with humility, acceptance (not defeatism) and *self-control*, is critical to our mental and emotional stability.

This control over her emotions and expectations, and the enduring patience she has embraced, enable her to move forward, to not get stuck in the unfairness of it all. In fact, the expectation of fairness can oftentimes be a distraction.

Of course it's not fair that Immy should face this circumstance at such a tender age. But she is, and she is doing it with self-control and grace.

CRITICAL FACTORS MAKING SELF-CONTROL A FOREVER SKILL:

- **In truth, all we can ever control is ourselves.**
- **Circumstances are ultimately less determinant of our results than our responses to them.**
- **A sense of control gives us focus and allows us to access our unique personal power.**

An oft-repeated maxim has it that we need to 'Play the cards we are dealt'.

Another quote making the internet rounds states,

> *You will continue to suffer if you have an emotional reaction to everything that is said to you. True power is sitting back and observing things with logic. True power is restraint. If words control you that means everyone else can control you. Breathe and allow things to pass.*

Controlling ourselves is one of the key skills we need to master as, ultimately, we are responsible for our actions (independent of our feelings). We are the navigator, the driver and the captain. We choose our mindset.

Learning how to manage ourselves is one of life's most essential skills and one we will always need. You can gain self-control if you:

1. Develop your self-awareness.

2. Understand that your emotions are feedback (and not always accurate).

3. Choose your mindset consciously.

4. Control your focus.

5. Control the controllable.

1 DEVELOP YOUR SELF-AWARENESS

It's tempting to try to ignore our foibles and hope no-one else notices. This is usually a mistake.

Far better, in our opinion, to take the sage advice inscribed in the *pronaos* (forecourt) of the Temple of Apollo at Delphi according to the Greek writer Pausanias in the second century: 'γνῶθι σεαυτόν', transliterated as *gnōthi seauton* or 'Know Thyself'.

One of the problems with a lack of self-awareness is precisely that we are quite literally unaware of both our weaknesses and also of the vulnerabilities that hide in our strengths.

In much of our consulting work with leaders and organisations around the world, we will typically conduct what we call an 'un-SWOT'.

Of course, the SWOT analysis is not our invention. In fact, it has been one of the most commonly used strategic tools in the twentieth and twenty-first centuries — applied to businesses and to individuals. However, our belief is that it is often incomplete and can actually facilitate a greater lack of strategy and self-awareness.

Let us explain. A traditional SWOT analysis has participants identify their Strengths, Weaknesses, Opportunities and Threats. Sounds simple enough, and oftentimes it is. However, in our observation, Strengths are usually category-generic (i.e. in a room filled with carpenters, being good with a hammer is essentially worthless), our Weaknesses are often assets in disguise, Opportunities that are easily identifiable will typically lead us into a highly competitive market that others have seen too, and Threats are probably best viewed as a chance to rise and lift our game.

In other words, every Strength casts a shadow and every Weakness has an upside. In the process of conducting our 'un-SWOT' we will have participants rank their strengths and weaknesses using a scale denoting their relative efficacy. We'll then have them explore the shadows cast and upsides available and then rank the influence they might exhibit.

The result we find on many occasions is that our Strengths may indeed be Net Weaknesses, while our Weaknesses might be Net Opportunities.

Self-control is understanding both sides of the equation and knowing what can undermine or propel us.

The point is that most of us rarely take the time to truly understand who we really are, the capabilities we have within us or the fabric of our characters.

In Plato's 'Apology', he quotes a speech Socrates gave at his trial: 'The unexamined life is not worth living.'

Framed another way, 'An examined life is *far more* worth living.'

2 UNDERSTAND THAT YOUR EMOTIONS ARE FEEDBACK (AND NOT ALWAYS ACCURATE)

Mark Mathews is a champion big wave surfer. Just to give you some sense of what a madman Mark is, the waves he surfs are measured metaphorically against the height of apartment buildings.

Mark shared the story of crashing into a coral reef and 'smashing his leg'. On waking up, he was told, 'The good news is we managed to save your leg. The bad news is, you will have a lifetime of pain, a slow recovery and you will never surf again.'

This sensitive framing caused him to spiral into a dark, miserable place. His recovery was agonisingly slow. Then one day, he received a request from a fan via Instagram, another patient in the same hospital, who wanted to pay Mark a visit. He couldn't say no (because his wife told him he couldn't).

When his fan, Jason, arrives, he is in a wheelchair, barely able to move, let alone walk; the result of a snowboarding accident that has kept him in hospital for a considerably longer time than Mark. Mark told us how in that moment he reframed his accident and, more importantly, his perceived unluckiness: 'I wasn't unlucky anymore. I was lucky.'

This kind of story plays out repeatedly in the lives of extraordinary people who rise up against trials time after time. Successful people create mental reframes that allow them to keep trying new things despite setbacks. To keep going in spite of logic that is tempting them to give up. They control the most powerful thing they have: their mind.

Obviously, even very successful people have times of doubt, days of inaction and even months where self-belief eludes them, but they also manage to create a mental story that supports them in trying again.

Our emotions are essentially feedback on our experience and environment. The problem that this presents us is that often that feedback is faulty, or at least not particularly useful. Essentially, we're running legacy emotional software that tends to process something like the idea of making a presentation to a boardroom of people with the same 'fear' response as encountering a pack of wolves in the wild.

What people like Mark teach us is that we should question the emotional feedback we are receiving and be willing to frame it in a more useful and helpful way.

3 CHOOSE YOUR MINDSET CONSCIOUSLY

Author and artist Dr Seuss in his final book advises us, 'You have brains in your head, you have feet in your shoes, you can steer yourself any direction you choose.'

We love this quote because it challenges an oft-held misconception. Mindset is regularly referred to as an attitude that winners are somehow blessed with, rather than a conscious choice and a skill we might cultivate.

This definition is quickly dismissed when we sit down with Major Matina Jewell (retired), one of the most decorated female officers in Australian military history.

Matina (Matti) Jewell is quite an inspiring human being, by her biography alone. She is the first army woman to qualify as a navy diver and to fast rope (what might be considered the extreme sport cousin to abseiling, without a safety harness) onto navy ships in the North Arabian Gulf. She has served alongside US Navy Seals in the Middle East, helped track down a notorious militia leader in the Solomon Islands and has successfully lobbied the UN to change processes to help save the lives of

Peacekeepers on UN missions around the world. All after facing incredible personal loss and trauma.

She talked to us about her choice of mindset in helping her get through the tragedy of losing her team mates during the 2006 Lebanon War, where she herself sustained career ending injuries including five fractured and crushed vertebrae and associated nerve damage. 'I was suffering post-traumatic stress, I couldn't get out of bed, I sat on the floor of the shower for hours.'

Rather than continuing to see her situation through a mindset of defeat, Matti chose a mindset that was open to change and growth. She used her experiences to challenge the way the Australian government treated veterans, to provide better support for those injured in the line of duty and to make a positive contribution by sharing her leadership and resilience lessons with audiences around the world.

It's a theme picked up by Lisa Ronson, the chief marketing officer at Tourism Australia. Lisa is the woman responsible for making sure Chris Hemsworth is on our screens in high rotation, spruiking the beauty of Australia while being the embodiment of the beauty of Australia. The world thanks you, Lisa. Thank you.

Lisa described mindset as a 'Conscious decision to see the best in a situation.'

Thinking further, she clarified that this is not being ignorant of the reality of the situation, but rather of being able to generate a useful sense of meaning around it. 'It's not about being blind,' she continued, 'but about being prepared and choosing how you manage your expectations.'

In other words, it's about demonstrating self-control over where your focus should go.

Hint: it should always go somewhere that gives you the biggest chance to create meaningful progress.

4 CONTROL YOUR FOCUS

Andrew Morello is a young entrepreneur and philanthropist who also just happens to be the first winner of *The Apprentice* Australia. We caught up with Andrew in a café across the road from his offices. He was holding court with what might best be described as an entourage hanging on his every word.

He reminded us that one of the most critical parts of controlling your focus is being conscious of the people you spend your time with, citing the old adage, 'You are the sum of the people you spend the most time with.'

Andrew is clear that choosing the correct focus is a lot easier to sustain when you are surrounded by a variety of people who challenge and support you. Andrew counselled us to not

> *hang around people who suck all the life, optimism and possibility out of you. There are people who try to keep you small. People who want less for you to make them feel better about themselves. Ignore criticism from people you don't like or respect.*

Some time ago, we were having dinner in Los Angeles with an old colleague and dear friend Andy Healy. Andy is a former advertising executive who now works as a scriptwriter in California.

We shared one of those evenings where time seems to evaporate. We talked about all of the things we were up to, the plans we were making and business opportunities we were exploring. We laughed. We ate. Plans for the extraordinary were discussed.

At the end of the evening Andy made an observation that has stuck with us since.

> *Usually when I catch up with old friends we talk about who we were and what we did. We connect over the past. But not us, we always talk about who we are becoming and where we are going. I love that.*

Do you have a network that moves you towards your aspirations? If not, get one!

Of course, choosing your focus applies to more than the people we spend our time with. Peter Sheahan, the chairman and CEO of Karrikins Group, a business-growth strategy consulting firm based in Denver, Toronto, Sydney and Auckland, shared with us that one of the top three skills he believes has helped him build his business was the ability to control his focus. He calls it discipline.

> *It's not so much working hard, but being able to select the work that will have the biggest impact. What's the highest value contribution I can make? Or if I only have an hour, what's the most valuable thing I can do?*

He told us it is ultimately about leverage. 'You need the ability to deselect as much as to select. To choose where to spend your time and energy.'

Control where you apply your focus strategically. Care about what you care about and care with as much gusto as you can.

5 CONTROL THE CONTROLLABLE

Obviously, we can't control everything. Trying to is exhausting, distracting and, frankly, unwise. Skilful people, however, understand the sense and logic in focusing on what they can control.

Libby Trickett has been a world record holder, an Olympic gold medallist and has won over 42 swimming medals on the world stage. She shared with us how much psychology is involved in elite sport and the lessons she learned along the way.

> *When you are a world champion, there is a lot of pressure. But you can't control everything. I learned to control the controllables. I can't control if someone else is going to swim out of their skin, I can only control my body and my preparation. So I focused on those things.*

Libby applied her focus on where she could exert the most control rather than on the distractions that were not only unhelpful, but beyond her power. For Libby, her controllables were food, sleep, training, rituals. We all have controllables in our lives, places where we can have the most impact and drive the most effective results.

And yet, so many of us waste our time, energy and attention on things that we cannot control, do not help us make progress or contribute to our ultimate success.

An example of this is Dr Adam Fraser's concept of the 'Third Space'. Simply put, the Third Space is about controlling how you transition from one environment to another in such a way that you create a decompression opportunity between circumstances that might require a completely different emotional energy.

This allows you to control your emotional state as you transition between the different physical and emotional spheres you operate in.

Adam applies this thinking to military veterans returning to civilian life, to salespeople transitioning from a negative sales call to the next and to corporate executives moving from 'business-psycho' to caring parent.

∞

Self-control is all about knowing who you are, what lifts you and what pushes your buttons, about identifying where your focus should be and choosing your mindset, but ultimately, it's about understanding what does lie within your control and your willingness to exercise that control. These things are timeless.

Self-control is ultimately about showing up ready to do the best you can. It is about minimising wasted emotion and distraction so you can get on with making the difference you want to make.

APPLICATION

FIVE STEPS FOR INCREASING YOUR SELF-CONTROL

1. Develop your self-awareness.
2. Understand that your emotions are feedback (and not always accurate).
3. Choose your mindset consciously.
4. Control your focus.
5. Control the controllable.

Resource management

Whether it's time, money, energy or people, all resources are finite, and managing them is critical to any success.

Kieran's ten-year-old daughter Darcy understands resource management. Kieran learned this last Halloween.

Darcy shared some candy-based business wisdom with her mother through a conversation that began with the observation, 'Mum, you know how companies charge people a small percentage for their services sometimes?'

Kieran responded, 'Yes', slightly concerned about where this might be heading.

'I did that for Halloween with my friends,' Darcy explained. 'They agreed that they wouldn't have been able to trick or treat in a street with so much candy if I had not invited them over. So I charged them a tax.'

Kieran, realising she was raising a Machiavellian, calmly inquired, 'Oh really?'

Darcy reassured her mother, 'Don't worry, just a small fee, one piece each.' Kieran was at once a proud mother (and just a little concerned).

What Darcy had realised at a very young age is that resources, assets and environments are limited and also that it is limitation that gives them value. This limitation and value must also be managed.

The same holds true in the authoring of a book, like this one, for instance. There is only so much time available for us to write and edit it and we, like most people, have more than one thing on. We are rarely in the same city, even the same country. This makes a capacity to manage our time and effort all the more valuable. In order to make a book like this happen, managing our time, focus and even the money we invest in the research we conduct is a critical component.

It's the same for you. Whatever you want to achieve in life or work, your ability to control your resources is important.

CRITICAL FACTORS MAKING RESOURCE MANAGEMENT A FOREVER SKILL:

- **With the exception of imagination, all other resources are finite.**
- **No-one ever has all they would like, so we need to have strategies to make what we have work.**
- **An inability to prioritise resources or make choices powerfully can lead to catastrophic failures.**

When we spoke with Jamie Pride, a serial entrepreneur and the author of *Unicorn Tears*, he explained that one of the key mistakes that start-ups make is to have 'too much money'. The problem, in Jamie's estimation, is that having too much capital in founding a business leads to sloppiness in decision making and increases the likelihood of procrastination and an unconscious unwillingness to demonstrate good judgement.

Of course, the resources we must manage come in all guises — money, energy, attention, raw materials, even people and ultimately the sustainability of the planet. Although of all of these, we believe management guru Peter Drucker nails it when he reminds us that 'Until we can manage time we can manage nothing else'.

While the substance and nature of the resources we manage may change as technological advances shift from mud to timber, brick, steel, graphene and whatever replaces graphene, for example, our capacity to make value-based judgement calls on how, where and when these resources are deployed is a skill we will need forever.

So how might you cultivate the skill of resource management?

1. Spend your resources wisely.

2. Place value on intangibles.

3. Create value through a useful frame of reference.

4. Don't just manage quantity, measure quality too.

5. Timing is … everything.

6. Assume a healthy margin of error.

1 SPEND YOUR RESOURCES WISELY

We all need (and will always need) the ability to spend wisely and strategically. Time, money, raw materials or any other finite must be carefully deployed.

Let's focus on the one resource that came up most frequently in our conversations as needed universally. The ability to manage money.

Financial acumen sounds like a business basic, but you would be surprised at just how many people are lacking this skill. From kids who know nothing about what to do with the wages they make from their first job (beyond buying calling credit) to start-ups that go broke because they cannot read a balance sheet to staff who have no concept that how they spend company money affects the bottom line. Not to mention leaders who outsource the responsibility for money to the finance department.

Financial acumen is both forever and crucial. It came up in many of our conversations. As Neil Plumridge of PwC told us, 'Very few people achieve success without a good basic understanding of financial literacy.'

Many of us do not have great money skills. According to a survey on consumer finances by the US Federal Reserve, a massive 48 per cent of current workers in the United States between the ages of 50 and 64 are on track to being poor when they reach retirement. A typical working family approaching retirement (with a head of house between 55 and 64) has on average $104 000 in retirement savings.

The situation is so dire that money guru Melissa Browne named her bestselling book *Unf*ck Your Finances*.

Melissa works with companies to help their people get smarter about money. Smart companies now realise that if their people are financially secure then they are less worried and distracted at work, which makes them more productive.

She told us her work is making money something we are less private and ashamed about ('You can talk about sex more readily than money.'), because our unwillingness to learn how to manage our resources is leaving us with considerably less to manage.

That said, resources are not always so tangible.

2 PLACE VALUE ON INTANGIBLES

We don't always value the intangibles as much as we should.

It is much easier to value, manage and account for resources when they are tangible: You can stocktake them, put them on a balance sheet and estimate their growth or volume.

What is harder to measure and manage is assets that have intangible value. Things such as personal energy, mental health, wellness, enthusiasm, trust, reputation, attention, focus and potential are just some of the important intangibles you have at your disposal.

They are incredibly valuable resources, yet many of us tend not to think of them that way. And we really should.

Lisa O'Neill's career ambition is to be a 'beam of light'. She is not far off of it, either. Hilarious, feisty and fabulous, she entertains audiences with comedic inspiration and dizzies them with huge volumes of energy.

She shared with us a conversation she had with a client who was booking her for an event. The client had massively increased the number of people in the room from the agreed number, and she wanted more money. The client was confused: 'But it's the same amount of time and the same content.' She replied, 'I don't work in time and content, I work in energy. That number of people takes so much more energy and so it will cost you more.'

While unconventional, she is absolutely right. We all trade in energy. No-one wants to work with or for a lacklustre person who is tired and jaded. Energy is one of the most important resources you have. It just happens to be intangible.

The key is knowing what intangibles you rely on to get results, and being ruthless, or at least strategic, about how you invest them.

If you spend these resources with the wrong people on the wrong tasks you may burn out, get bitter, resent the world and never achieve what you might have if you spent them wisely.

Plenty of people have gone that way. You'll typically find them loitering near water coolers in corporate offices, sucking the enthusiasm right out of newbies who arrive full of those intangibles. 'You'll learn. Just wait. You'll soon have that self-belief beaten out of you!' Or, as a woman kindly informed us one day while running a workshop for a government department, 'You guys are great, so inspiring — you make me want to care. But to be honest, I am just counting down the days until I retire.'

Counting down days until the end is no way to live. It never has been.

Treat your intangibles as you would your tangibles:

1. Work out what intangibles you rely on to keep you motivated and moving.

2. Be conscious of where and when you spend them.

3. Notice where you are spending too much of them.

4. Try and remove any inefficiencies. (People, tasks, roadblocks.)

5. Know what you need to replenish or build them, and design it into your life.

Stephen Hawking taught us by example that life is ultimately about making the most out of what you've got.

3 CREATE VALUE THROUGH A USEFUL FRAME OF REFERENCE

At the beginning of every year, Kieran, along with Janine Garner, who we introduced you to in earlier chapters, runs a New Year kick-off program called 'The Year of You'. It's a way for people to shift from making New Year's resolutions (which, according to a 2017 US News study, revealed an approximate 80 per cent failure rate by the second week of February), to one of shaping the year around achievable strategic objectives.

One of the key processes Kieran enlists in this program is a simple 'Year on a Page' exercise.

One of the reasons we fail in achieving our New Year's resolutions is that at the beginning of a year, 365 days seems like a significant period of time. To counter this, Kieran very quickly creates a frame of reference that generates both urgency and action.

'It is not a year,' Kieran suggests. 'It's fifty-two Saturdays.'

Kieran then extends the thinking to other parts of the audience's lives, suggesting your kids' childhood only provides you with a maximum of 18 vacation opportunities with them before they become adults and no longer want to hang out with you. 'This,' she explains, 'is based on the presumption that you only have one holiday a year, and, given they probably won't remember much before the age of four, you've really only got fourteen.'

It's tough love, but it helps people appreciate the time they have available, whether it's a year or 18 years, in a way they had not before.

We apply a similar line of thinking to our own business based on work we've done with Matt Church and Peter Cook, whom we referenced earlier in the book. We don't think in terms of calendar or financial years, we think in terms of quarters, which are 12 weeks long, giving us just 90 days to design, prototype, test and execute a new business offering in the market.

In other words, we frame time in a way that makes it useful and actionable.

A capacity to choose a frame of reference that inspires urgency and action is critical to making us appreciate time, money, energy and even tangible resources.

One of the reasons we avoid this kind of prioritisation exercise is that it can often be uncomfortable to consider how limited our resources are. Even our very lives are an example of a limited resource. We may not like to think about it, but we are all hurtling towards our eventual demise. Not a cheery thought but hopefully quite motivating!

Google has actually developed a clock within their Chrome platform that runs a countdown on your life based on average life expectancy. Apple Watch has a Life Clock app that works like a reverse activity tracker. Rather than giving you a readout of actions you did in the past, it tracks all your actions, both positive and negative, throughout the day, and constantly adjusts the estimate of when you're going to put foot to bucket!

If your curiosity is piqued, the average life span of human beings in the United States is 28 654 days (or 687 660 hours, or 41 259 600 minutes, or 2 475 576 000 seconds). Tick, tock, tick, tock.

In other words, choose a frame that encourages you to manage your resources wisely.

4 DON'T JUST MANAGE QUANTITY, MEASURE QUALITY TOO

Quality, of course, is relative.

After the end of the American Civil War, millions of dollars in Confederate currency was worthless. The same holds true for expensive wine that has corked (a term for a wine that has become contaminated with cork taint).

Of course, the quality of our people, of community engagement, of our brand value and even what our balance sheet refers to as assets can fluctuate and change.

Getting this wrong can be catastrophic. A lesson Tsar Nicholas II learned at the end of a firing squad's rifles.

The head of the Russian Imperial Romanov family had many failings, including a lack of military experience and strategic skills, an obvious blind spot in terms of whose company his wife was keeping, and poor decision making. This poor decision making led to escalating tensions between himself and the government, resulting in increased hardship for the general population, including civilians and soldiers.

In other words, despite having incredible resources, wealth and dynastic wisdom at his command, he was fatally unaware of the temperature of the culture over which he presided. It was a lack of quality in resources, not quantity, that would ultimately cost his family so dearly.

This is a pattern of behaviour we see play out in modern corporations and government departments. Leaders who are either too arrogant or too ignorant of how change is affecting the relative value of their product, their people or the sector in which they operate very soon find out that quantity does not equal quality.

What can we learn from this? Principally, that traditional stocktakes or asset audits are incomplete methodologies for managing resources. The nature and value of resources will change over time, and occasionally overnight, if we are not vigilant.

This is a difficult process for an algorithm to predict, partly because of the fickle and fractious nature of human behaviour and fashion, but also because what is seemingly unrelated can take us by surprise.

To steal a line from the Monty Python team, 'No-one expects the Spanish Inquisition.' And likewise, the taxi industry, despite its global scale, time in market and considerable marketplace, failed to predict Uber, and the hotel industry failed to predict Airbnb.

5 CHOOSE YOUR TIMING ... WISELY

It's well understood that timing is everything in comedy, and even drama. Introducing the wrong fact or character can completely throw off an audience's suspension of disbelief.

In fact, in 2018, the inclusion of Professor McGonagall on the big screen in J K Rowling's *Fantastic Beasts: The Crimes Of Grindelwald,* angered fans to the point that they tweeted such gems as:

> *I know JKR is bad at math but this is ridiculous. How is the biography she wrote 4 years ago about McGonagall and how she was a student under Dumbledore fits with Mcgonagall being a professor in 1927?!? @Meliahipics*

> *If McGonagall started Hogwarts in 1947, she would've been born in 1935, but she makes an appearance as a young adult in Fantastic Beasts 2 which is set in 1927? @tomfev*

> *'McGonagall confirmed in Fantastic Beasts 2' Did she go back in time? @_potterhead7*

Oh for a time when our mistakes were mostly private!

However, timing is not confined to the world of drama and entertainment, but is a critical consideration in any undertaking.

This understanding has led to such business strategies as 'Just in time delivery', which allows the fulfilment of raw-material orders from suppliers to directly coordinate with the production schedules of end users and with customer orders.

This means companies increase efficiency and decrease waste by receiving goods only as they need them for the production process. This, in turn, reduces inventory costs but also requires producers to accurately forecast demand.

Marketing is another business function that is largely driven by resource management timing. Running an attack ad the day after the death of a competitor's founder will win you few friends, and product launches are almost always designed to correlate with favourable social and market conditions.

However, this understanding of timing in resource management is just as important in more everyday applications such as building a house, where the different trades and contractors must be coordinated, not only so they show up to perform their services in the correct order, but also that the right supplies and building materials will be available on site.

The same holds true for anyone who has ever tried to follow a recipe more complicated than fried eggs. Get the order and timing of the ingredients wrong and you're ordering pizza.

So beyond simply understanding what we have and what condition it is in, understanding when a resource must be deployed is a critical function of resource management.

6 ASSUME A HEALTHY MARGIN OF ERROR

Having worked with organisations and small businesses around the world, one of the most damaging omissions that we see in business plans and sales projections is too narrow a margin of error.

We're all for being optimistic, but hope is not a strategy.

In other words, assume that things will go wrong, that product will spoil, that service staff will call in sick (or fail to show up without notice), that warehousing software will for some reason stop speaking to sales software and that your best people, the ones you count on, will be poached and offered more money and better conditions than you can match. Because: Things. Will. Go. Wrong.

The issue is not that things go wrong, it's that we make no provision for when things go wrong. And managing resources is one of those skills where things going wrong can cost us economically and commercially.

∞

In the digital economy, our customers, clients and communities are not lacking options. If you don't have what they want in stock, they can reach into their pockets and check availability with almost every supplier on the planet in seconds.

What this all means is, yes, many of the resource management functions will be outsourced and automated by algorithms run by artificial intelligence and actioned by robots working 24/7.

However, judgement and strategy used to navigate a world that is abundant in unpredictability have always been a critical function of control in human societies, and though the resources we manage might change, the need for resource management will remain.

APPLICATION

FIVE STEPS FOR INCREASING YOUR RESOURCE MANAGEMENT

1. Spend your resources wisely.
2. Place value on intangibles.
3. Create value through a useful frame of reference.
4. Don't just manage quantity, measure quality too.
5. Timing is … everything.
6. Assume a healthy margin of error.

Order

12

**Whether we seek consensus or mould consensus,
the need for social order will remain.**

In *Lord of the Flies,* William Golding speculated what would happen if society degenerated into childish unregulated anarchy. Spoiler alert: Piggy gets killed in a frenetic unleashing of emotion and groupthink.

In fact many modern dystopian novels explore the breakdown of society as we know it. Usually, the downtrodden win and the evil overlords get their comeuppance (but we suspect this is probably a function of what sells books and movie tickets).

In reality, every revolution, whether social, commercial or psychological, is almost immediately followed by an establishment of new rules and acceptable behaviours. Order never truly goes away; it simply morphs into the New Order.

Throughout history, our societies and communities have been held together by a collection of loose and more formal agreements that are designed, at least in part, to prevent us from taking advantage of, stealing from, injuring and even killing each other.

Hardly surprising, given that society is made up of a complex series of interdependent people, places and processes. We have always had to navigate and balance the often conflicting demands for individual freedoms and shared safety and security. A binary system that is only exaggerated by our current two party–dominated system of government.

The truth is, the predominance of one negates the other, and, as both have their virtues, the debate rages on.

This means that those who can successfully navigate societal norms, understand how to work with them and push them where needed will always be essential.

CRITICAL FACTORS MAKING ORDER A FOREVER SKILL:

- **As long as human beings decide to co-exist in large social structures, we will need to negotiate a consensus of acceptable behaviour.**
- **Not all of us are willing to play by the rules and abide by these community conventions.**
- **Just occasionally, for the good of the many over the desires of the few, social order must be enforced and perhaps even forced.**

Of course, this raises the uncomfortable question: 'Just whose social order is being enforced, and who decided this was the correct one?' This question echoes throughout the entire history of our species and we suspect it is not going away any time soon, if at all.

Of course, this need goes beyond the realm of government, policing, the military and the courts, as even in our families, our community clubs and corporate organisations, standards of behaviour are always being set, met or unmet and re-negotiated.

As stated in part II, we know a diversity of people and opinions makes us collectively smarter and that this diversity enriches our lives, our families and friendships and, of course, our dining options.

However, it is also worth being aware that these conditions do not always occur naturally, voluntarily or without resistance, protest and even violence.

This makes a capacity to reach consensus, to shape behaviour and to establish boundaries for human behaviour that allow us to coexist peacefully a Forever Skill.

You can build this capacity if you:

1. Establish a sense of certainty.

2. Strive for absolute clarity.

3. Hold yourself and others accountable.

4. Establish social order and convention.

5. Be values focused.

1 ESTABLISH A SENSE OF CERTAINTY

One of our favourite quotes from Winston Churchill is the following:

Never give in—never, never, never, never, in nothing great or small, large or petty, never give in except to convictions of honour and good sense. Never yield to force; never yield to the apparently overwhelming might of the enemy.

That is pretty unequivocal. It's hard to imagine the average British 'Tommy' hearing Churchill's inspiring words in 1941 and wondering, 'So is that three, or four nevers before we give in?'

The truth of the matter was, Churchill personally had no such access to certainty. The United States did not join the Allied Coalition until December 1941 and the German military was, frankly, doing a good job of holding British soldiers at bay while demolishing London's East End from the air.

This is a critical distinction. It is not a leader's place to be certain, but rather to create a *sense of certainty* in their populace, organisation or team.

In fact, much of the discord we are experiencing in modern Western democracies is driven, in part, by the lack of certainty large parts of their populations are experiencing.

In most of the Western world, religion is in decline, creating a moral or ethical uncertainty. The Western world is also far more multicultural than it once was, which destabilises certainty around a shared sense of identity and common beliefs. And as heavy industries such as manufacturing and agriculture are either outsourced to developing economies or automated by robotics, uncertainties about income and employment security are fuelling widespread fear and discontent.

In other words, a lack of security unsettles social norms and undermines social and interpersonal order. Of course, this shows up in all institutions.

According to an article in the journal *Paediatric Child Health* called 'The Impact of Poverty on Educational Outcomes for Children', a range of studies has shown that children of lower socioeconomic status tend to achieve poorer results academically. They 'score lower in communication and vocabulary skills, knowledge of numbers, ability to copy and recognise symbols, concentration, and teamwork and cooperative play'.

Additional research conducted by the Society for Research in Child Development also found that children from low-income families received less positive parenting and had higher levels of cortisol, which has been associated with lower levels of cognitive development. Much of this contemporary research echoes the findings made in 1966 by Johns Hopkins University sociologist James S Coleman in his *Equality of Educational Opportunity* report.

What these and other studies exploring educational outcomes are suggesting is that an uncertain family and home life dramatically affects academic performance in children.

This is not entirely surprising, as a child forced to negotiate survival needs has rather more important things on their mind than trigonometry. Something all of us can relate to. If we are experiencing stress or duress it is harder to concentrate on daily tasks.

Of course, this also shows up in our businesses and organisations, as teams and employees gravitate to leaders who convey the most certainty, customer buy from salespeople with the greatest conviction, and cultures that embody a sense of certainty about their vision and mission attract and retain more motivated and higher performing team members.

In other words, order has its origins in the creation of certainty.

2 STRIVE FOR ABSOLUTE CLARITY

'Of course we obey the rules. Now, what are the rules?'

It sounds like a line from a Marx Brothers film, and yet versions of this conversation play out in all aspects of our lives: in schools, in families, in organisations and even in personal relationships.

If we want to establish codes of conduct and behaviour, clarity is critical.

Ben Hunt-Davis tells the story of the Great Britain Men's Rowing Eight winning gold at the 2000 Sydney Olympics in his book *Will It Make the Boat Go Faster?*

To us, the book's title is a perfect example of what we call a 'guiding question'. A guiding question is outcome-focused and delivers a ruthlessness of clarity around behaviour and action. Importantly, people can answer a guiding question for themselves and adjust their actions and priorities accordingly.

Not only is the objective — speed — pretty obvious from this guiding question, it also sets up a framework for success that removes doubt and ambiguity.

What's also interesting about this book is Ben's idea of 'layered goals'. It's not just *one* thing that will make 'the boat go faster' (or your business grow or your fitness improve — feel free to add personal ambitions as you see fit), but rather that everything they do, every bite-sized goal or task, must contribute to making the boat go faster.

What's critically important in this observation, and what makes it more than another poorly transferable sport metaphor, is that it encourages self-correcting behaviour.

With a clear guiding question, I don't need to check in with management, Mum and Dad, the 'authorities' or my peers to know if I'm doing the right things or not. It's in the title!

We have to make the parameters around desired and acceptable behaviour clear. We must remove doubt, absolutely. When we do this we reduce the need to micromanage or police every aspect of behaviour. We allow people to control themselves in accordance with the goal.

3 HOLD YOURSELF AND OTHERS ACCOUNTABLE

When you think of business case studies about establishing clear metrics and measures to monitor performance and drive accountability, you don't often think of the flamboyant frontman for Van Halen during the 1970s and 1980s, David Lee Roth. And yet, here we are.

We're all familiar with the kind of outrageous requests high-profile celebrities tend to make in their riders; 12 perfect long-stemmed white roses with the prickles removed and arranged pleasingly in a frosted glass vase, a bottle of absinthe stolen from a Romani market trader, and the like.

While touring in the 1970s and 1980s, Van Halen were no different.

Their rider included some obvious inclusions such as a fresh fruit platter of apples, oranges, grapes, pears, melons, kiwi fruit and bananas. Hot drinks included hot brewed coffee (not instant, which is fair enough), hot water for tea, Lipton tea bags, herbal tea bags, Tupelo honey, 12 lemons, cream and sugar. And under 'Munchies' — potato chips with assorted dips, nuts, pretzels, M&M's (Warning: absolutely no brown ones), 12 Reese's peanut butter cups and 12 assorted Dannon yoghurts on ice.

The most critical element on the list, as you may have identified, is the M&M's — more specifically, the request for 'Absolutely no brown ones'.

'Big deal,' you may be thinking. 'Prima donnas!'

As it turns out, it is rather a big deal. A touring rock show has a lot of moving pieces and Van Halen had more pieces than most — pyrotechnics, lighting, sound, staging that moved. That's a lot to monitor and creates multiple breakage points in the system. Far more than the band could actively check.

The M&M's became a kind of 'Canary in the coalmine' for the band. As the frontman said to *Business Insider* in 2012,

> *If I came backstage, having been one of the architects of this lighting and staging design, and I saw brown M&M's on the catering table, then I guarantee the promoter had not read the contract rider, and we would have to do a serious line check [of the entire stage setup].*

To establish order, we need to set up systems and checks that hold ourselves accountable to our word and others accountable to shared expectations.

4 ESTABLISH SOCIAL ORDER AND CONVENTION

It would be remiss to have any discussion about order in the context of control as a Forever Skill without interviewing any legal professionals.

So we sat down with former barrister, acting judge and retired public prosecutor Nick Cowdery.

What Nick shared with us is that, despite basing arguments and judgements on proven facts and well-articulated laws and using past precedent to guide current application, right and wrong are often less black and white than we might expect.

Part of this was informed by changes in community standards. Often the law was slow to catch up to where society's values had shifted. Examples of this might be the changes to same-sex marriage laws, the changing attitudes (in the community and in law enforcement) to abortion and community attitudes to drug taking and voluntary assisted dying.

Nick suggested that much decision making came down to: the agendas of those presenting themselves before the courts; the politicians and committees making appointments; and the information that officers of the courts are privy to at the time of making their decisions. In other words, good judgement required good judgement.

Given this experience, Nick advised us, 'Develop your bullshit detection skills. This is largely a result of life experience, hopefully as broad as is possible. There are still too many citizens uncritically accepting BS from sources they trust, but should not.'

Nick suggested that everyone has an agenda, not necessarily a nefarious one, but certainly people in all relationships have a purpose in what they are telling you and a desired outcome they are working towards.

'You need to learn to read people's agendas, to understand what a win looks like for them and consider self-critically whether you are being manipulated or not.'

He suggested five steps for making order-based decisions under pressing conditions:

1. Assess what information you have.

2. Generate options for how your decision might play out.

3. Make assessments on positives and negatives.

4. Refer to your own experience or engage those who have more.

5. Use deadlines to spur action and avoid perfectionism.

5 BE VALUES FOCUSED

If we assess the words that we heard repeated most often throughout the interview portion of our research, 'values' would be right at the top of the list. Although, as we discovered with words such as 'leadership' and 'resilience', single words seem to have numerous definitions.

One of the people we've turned to over the years for advice on our business concerns is Tony Harris. Tony has built and exited multiple businesses, and yet, despite having a finance background and a clearly commercial streak, he is someone others also look to as a community leader and whose council they seek on making business and life work harmoniously.

'All business is the business of relationships, at the end of the day!' Tony kicked off our interview with his infectious enthusiasm. 'In fact, so is everything in life.'

This led us into a conversation about the importance of building values-based businesses and communities. 'Ultimately, it's all about respect. Not agreement, but respect.'

Tony very much subscribes to the ethos that success is better when shared. But this is not a function of softness, but rather something Tony sees as critical to community building: 'The risk, I think, is that we might lose our ability to communicate in multiple directions. Technology has us all set to "broadcast".'

If we're not actually engaging in communication with different people, in different circumstances, having different life experiences to us, then all we're really demonstrating is that we're not interested in them.

'If you want people to buy from you or follow you or be interested in you, you'd better be able to demonstrate that you're interested in them.'

What Tony was alluding to was that the idea of order, whether social, organisational or even familial, boils down to an agreed set of values: laws, rules and conventions around behaviour are simply an attempt to codify what we believe to be true.

∞

Throughout history, an ability to agree on codes of conduct has been critical to ensuring harmonious family and community life. As the scale of our concept of family, kin and society has increased from familial to tribal to national and even global, this ability will not only continue to be essential, its importance will only increase as we become more interconnected and interdependent. This makes the ability to assert and apply order a Forever Skill.

APPLICATION

FIVE STEPS FOR INCREASING ORDER

1. Establish a sense of certainty.
2. Strive for absolute clarity.
3. Hold yourself and others accountable.
4. Establish social order and convention.
5. Be values focused.

Implementation

13

'Implementation beats oration.'
Aesop

Bronnie Ware is an Australian care giver who worked in palliative care. Or, in her words, with 'those who had gone home to die'.

She looked after people in the last three to 12 weeks of their lives. During that time, she recorded their dying wisdom and shared their regrets, in the hope that we all might learn from them, in a blog she created called Inspiration and Chai.

The blog gathered so much attention that she collated her observations into a book called *The Top Five Regrets of the Dying*. The book became a bestseller and has been translated into 29 languages. The film rights were optioned. This changed not only the lives of the people all over the world who read it, but also her own.

The 'most common regret of all' of the dying, according to her blog, was, 'I wish I'd had the courage to live a life true to myself, not the life others expected of me.'

> *When people realise that their life is almost over and look back clearly on it, it is easy to see how many dreams have gone unfulfilled. Most people had not honoured even a half of their dreams and had to die knowing that it was due to choices they had made, or not made. It is very important to try and honour at least some of your dreams along the way.*

Bronnie took action: she created a blog and wrote a book. What she implemented with the knowledge she had gained changed everything.

There are thousands of care givers all around the world who work with the dying. All of these would have heard the same regrets and had the same opportunity to access the wisdom of hindsight. But they didn't. They probably read Bronnie's book and thought, 'I could've written that.' They're right, they probably could have. But critically, Bronnie *did!*

Implementation is the key.

Reflecting on her success, Bronnie shared that she believed, 'Courage is the greatest tool for bringing our dreams into reality,' adding, 'Courage is often the pedal that accelerates us from ideas to action.'

We all have unrealised ideas in our heads, possibilities that are yet to become realities scribbled on scraps of paper and in Moleskines: half-finished projects, designs for inventions, plot lines for novels and 'big plans' we'll get to one day or some day. However, as the online meme goes, '"Someday" isn't a day of a week'.

Of course, dreams are wonderful, but they don't ultimately count. What matters in the end is what we implement: the actions we are prepared to take and the dreams we are willing to bring into reality. It has always been this way. History books are full of those who completed or at least tried. Those who kept their dreams hidden are seldom recorded. This makes implementation our 12th Forever Skill.

CRITICAL FACTORS MAKING IMPLEMENTATION A FOREVER SKILL:

- **Intent is cheap; what matters is action.**
- **An ability to be decisive and execute is a fundamental skill of leadership.**
- **Performance and action drive engagement, not the other way round.**

There is a seemingly endless supply of motivational quotes that remind us of the importance of the capacity to implement:

'The most effective way to do it, is to do it.' — Amelia Earhart

'If you wait, all that happens is that you get older.' — Mario Andretti

'To think is easy. To act is difficult. To act as one thinks is the most difficult.' — Johann Wolfgang Von Goethe

'My husband always tells me that I'm the most unrelenting person he's ever met, and it's true. If I make a commitment to something I will stick to it no matter what.' — Jenny Craig

'Well done is better than well said.' — Benjamin Franklin

'And the trouble is if you don't risk anything, you risk more.' — Erica Jong

'Action is the foundational key to all success.' — Pablo Picasso

'My whole career has been … getting ahead by small ugly steps.' — Joan Rivers

The list is almost endless, and yet, despite all of the aphorisms and incitements to take action, a capacity to implement is one of the Forever Skills we still need to develop.

How do might we improve our ability to implement?

1. Limit your options.
2. Build engagement by starting and finishing.
3. Hack your nature.
4. Develop commercial acumen (then back yourself).
5. Detach from the outcome.

1 LIMIT YOUR OPTIONS

In 2000, psychologists Sheena Iyengar and Mark Lepper published a study that suggested that sometimes *more* isn't always *better*. The study involved giving people a lot of choice or a little choice.

The researchers decided to conduct their experiment in a specialty grocery store after Sheena noticed that she would often walk out of the store with nothing, despite spending a great deal of time visiting and browsing.

So, along with Mark, she set up a jam display and swapped out the number of jams on display every hour and then observed what happened.

The more jam, the more people stopped (60 per cent). Less jam meant fewer people stopped (40 per cent). However, the second group were more likely to buy. In the end, out of those who encountered the larger selection, only 3 per cent purchased, while those who engaged with the smaller display converted to purchase by 30 per cent.

When they factored in the likelihood of people stopping in the first place, they calculated that fewer choices tended to mean people were six times more likely to buy.

We like a little choice. But too much can be paralysing and we end up making no choice at all.

This 'choice overload' shows up in other parts of the human experience also.

Recent research out of Caltech, published in the journal *Nature Human Behaviour* had similar findings. They even mapped human brain function to track the effects.

Colin Camerer, the author of the study, said,

> *The idea is that the best out of 12 is probably rather good, while the jump to the best out of 24 is not a big improvement. Essentially, our eyes are bigger than our stomachs. When we think about how many choices we want, we may not be mentally representing the frustrations of making the decision.*

What we can learn from these experiments is that decisions (and implementation) are difficult enough without exacerbating the problem by adding too many choices.

Of course, our choices are infinite, or as near as. The trick is narrowing them down so that we do not become paralysed by procrastination and perfectionism. We have to learn to quickly eliminate some choices so we can actually choose!

The truth is, we become more decisive, and better at implementation, by making decisions, and it seems one of the most important factors in making decisions is in limiting our options so that choice becomes more achievable.

2 BUILD ENGAGEMENT BY STARTING AND FINISHING

Joe Sabah reminds us that 'You don't have to be great to start, but you have to start to be great.'

If you want to get fit, walk to the corner today. Tomorrow you can walk to the next corner, and so on.

If you want to sleep more, go to bed five minutes earlier tonight, then five minutes earlier the next night and so on, just as our friend Professor James Arvanitakis advised us. Over coffee and conversations about how small shifts in culture and behaviour amplify, James told us that if he chose to go to bed significantly early one night, the next night he would be wide awake. So he stopped doing that. Instead he did it gradually, five minutes at a time.

In other words, it's not the scale of the commitment that most informs success, but the commitment to beginning and taking repeated action, however small.

An interesting example of this in the modern business world is the rise of the 'side hustle'. As the barriers to founding a business, setting up a distribution network and creating backend accounts receivable and accounting have diminished as a result of the digital revolution, many of us have embraced a modern method for starting a business, charity or cause in a relatively safe way.

According to a 2018 bankrate.com report, almost four in 10 Americans (37 per cent) have a side hustle. This includes *more than half* of Millennials.

Of course, many side hustles have become people's full-time hustles. Apple, Etsy, UnderArmour, Groupon, Unsplash, WeWork, Oculus or Sal Khan's Khan Academy are all examples of this.

And while starting matters, so does completing. Unfortunately, having the tenacity and drive to follow through is remarkably rare.

Just ask any parent whose home is littered with evidence of short-lived interests and endeavours: guitars, recorders, ice skates, tutus, football boots and 'parent tended' pet rabbits and so on.

Of course, it isn't just our kids. Half-finished projects litter homes and offices all over the world. A survey by ratedpeople.com suggests that 14 million households in Britain are living with an unfinished home project.

The skill of finishing is just as crucial as beginning. The ability to stay the course, to keep going and not be distracted by the new or the immediate very much distinguishes between those who succeed and those who simply dream about it.

So ask yourself:

- 'What is the first thing I need to do to get me on the way?'
- 'What is the most important thing I can do to progress my project right now?'
- 'What will be required of me to complete it?'

3 HACK YOUR NATURE

Many of us spend a great deal of time either revving ourselves up to be more motivated or else beating ourselves up for not being more disciplined.

It's as if we think there is something essentially wrong in human nature, and in us.

So let's just put that theory to rest, shall we?

In a 2015 paper titled 'Is Exercise Really Medicine? An Evolutionary Perspective', Daniel Lieberman, an expert in human evolutionary biology, suggests that 'It is natural and normal to be physically lazy.'

Daniel explains that it was necessary, from an evolutionary perspective, for our ancestors to conserve energy, as the food they consumed was not equal to the calories expended in gathering or hunting that food.

So if you were looking for a reason to justify your sense of laziness, look no further!

However, a more serious reading of the Lieberman's research and that of others in his field suggests that, rather than giving in to laziness, we would be better to 'hack' our natures, or at least work with them.

In our experience, design beats discipline. In other words, while motivation and discipline might be productive in the short term, they are unsustainable when it comes to real behavioural change.

We know this to be true from our own experience as human beings.

Suppose you have to catch a flight early in the morning. What do you do?

Do you motivate yourself and assume a zen-like discipline, trusting your internal body clock to raise you, rested and inspired, at the appropriate time? Or, like most of us, do you set your alarm clock? Likely you place it on the other side of the room so you have to physically get out of bed to stop it ringing, thus hacking your tendency to hit the snooze button.

This is hacking our nature in action. Rather than assuming our laziness or desire to conserve energy is an evolutionary mistake, consider how we might design processes, systems and habits with the reality of our natures in mind.

Kieran has a sock hack. Not because she is uber efficient but because, when it comes to domestic chores, she falls a little short. A lot short!

Rather than lamenting her lack of laundry-folding prowess, she decided only to buy one type of sock so they never need matching again. (Steal this idea at will. You are all welcome!)

Our friend Matt Church sleeps in his Lululemon training gear so that he feels compelled to exercise in the morning. He says that the worst part of going for a run is taking your warm clothes off and changing on a cold morning. So he takes that barrier out of the equation. 'Besides, I am unable to get past the personal shame of having to take my exercise gear off without exercising!' he adds.

What this all means is that if we want to master implementation (and we do), we would be wise to stop beating ourselves up and, instead, work with who we are. Our chances of success are much increased by accepting the reality of human nature as opposed to trying to unpack 65 million years of evolution with a trite affirmation such as, 'I am a magnificent snowflake filled with the infinite potential of the universe and I apply my genius to manifesting, with abundance, a consciousness of all humanity.'

4 DEVELOP COMMERCIAL ACUMEN (THEN BACK YOURSELF)

One of the greatest barriers to implementation is self-doubt. We spend a great deal of time admiring the successes of others and assume that they must possess some special ability or character trait that we are somehow missing.

Growing up and attending university, we would look up to successful businesspeople, C-suite executives and corporate board members and think to ourselves, 'One day, we might know just a fraction of what they do.' Of course, after almost thirty years of consulting to boards and leadership teams, and having sat on a few boards ourselves, we soon realised, 'They're all making it up too!!!'

This discovery should be seen as permission to not hold yourself back.

Rather, we all need to develop commercial acumen in order to survive in a competitive world. But then we need to back ourselves to make intelligent decisions, even in the face of extraordinary challenges.

Karen Merricks (with her husband, Roy) has built a multimillion-dollar travel business called MTA Travel. However, more important than the success of the business itself is the success of their model, which was revolutionary when they conceived of it over two decades ago:

> *Twenty years ago when we had a family we decided that there must be a better way. I thought if we wanted this other people must want it too. We risked everything. There was no Plan B!*

They created a business model where travel agents could serve their clients and customers with greater flexibility, working from their own homes or office spaces rather than being tied to a desk in a main street office or shopping mall.

Karen and Roy's insight proved correct. But what was more important was their willingness to implement and adjust as necessary.

What they discovered was that other people, especially women, wanted to be there for their families. They wanted to be able to earn money on their own terms. They wanted the freedom and flexibility that working for themselves could offer them.

Karen's insight into the mindset of mum-and-dad operators was spot-on and, with hard work, vision, a huge amount of empathy and a bucketload of kindness, they have built a trailblazing business that gives people the chance to work in a way that aligns with the other parts of their lives.

Karen's business success and the contribution she has made to those who have flocked to her banner required a true commercial acumen. She didn't simply hang her shingle and launch another generic travel business, she reinvented the industry by building a completely new business model.

Through this new business model, Karen has helped hundreds of parents raise their kids on their terms and share their passion for travel at the same time.

As savvy as Karen and Roy have become as businesspeople, what was more determinant of their success was a willingness to launch, to ship, to back themselves.

5 DETACH FROM THE OUTCOME

In the year 2000, Dan, who was at the time a particularly awful public speaker, began a world tour as a stand-up comedian with 30 minutes of material and four months' experience. Three years later, he was bulletproof and performing on stages around the United States, the UK, Europe and Australia.

Key in this success was a willingness to detach from the outcome.

In the initial stages of his comedy career, it's probably true to say that Dan was 'uber-attached'. He was tormented by thoughts such as, 'What if they don't laugh? What if I get heckled? What if I forget my material?'

All incredibly valid fears, as they were situations that showed up with disappointing regularity.

However, over time, Dan realised that he wasn't actually performing for the audience; he was performing because he loved it. This allowed him to revel in the moment, independent of the audience's expectations or reactions, and with this detachment came confidence and competency.

In fact, Dan's adoption of detachment became so ingrained that he would walk onto the stage reminding himself, 'They laugh, or they don't laugh, this is for *me!*'

It's important here to make a distinction between being detached and not caring — although oftentimes a little of the latter can give you a bit of swagger.

∞

Motivational speakers often enquire of their audiences, 'What would you do if you knew you couldn't fail?' We think that might be the wrong question. Clearly, we are all going to fail on the road to excellence, and deluding ourselves is hardly a strategy.

A better question, one that might actually drive us to implement what matters to us, is, 'What would make you feel more alive, independent of the opinion of others or outside metrics of success, and why haven't you begun it?'

To implement successfully, to enjoy the process and be engaged by it, we need to get out of our own way. Or, rather, to enlist our own natures in supporting us in the process.

By working with who we are, by developing a business acumen based on the value our work will provide, by limiting our options, making decisions and detaching from the outcome, we allow ourselves to move from the conceptual to the tangible.

As Goethe said, 'Boldness has genius, power and magic in it.' Old wisdom, but as relevant now and tomorrow as it was then.

APPLICATION

FIVE STEPS FOR INCREASING YOUR
IMPLEMENTATION

1. Limit your options.
2. Build engagement by starting and finishing.
3. Hack your nature.
4. Develop commercial acumen (then back yourself).
5. Detach from the outcome.

CONCLUSION

'Everyone thinks of changing the world,
but no one thinks of changing himself.'

Leo Tolstoy

You've reached the end of this book, but we would hate you to think of it as an end. Rather, it is an invitation to embrace the future by developing the skills that will always matter.

The need for the skills we have gathered and shared in this book is unending. This is their ultimate power. Of course, these are not the only 12 Forever Skills. We identified many skills that had to be clustered, intimated or even omitted, or else you would be reading forever!

We hope you will also identify your own Forever Skills. That you will share these 12, plus your own, with your communities, companies, teams, families and kids (and even us — we'd love to hear from you). That the knowledge accumulated through lifetimes of experience will continue to help us all navigate the future.

We ask you to talk about the idea of Forever Skills with those around you. That you pass on this book and the skills you have gleaned to others. Debate what is evergreen and eternally powerful. Decide the things worth keeping in your company, team or family. And the next time someone hyperventilates about the changes hurtling towards us, calmly provide a little perspective so that they might see all Three Spheres of Change, not just one.

There is so much that is changing, so much that needs changing and much that is unchanging.

1. *What's changing?* A great amount. In researching this book, what also became abundantly apparent is just how much of what is changing will ultimately sit beyond our control (despite 'control' being one of the three clusters of Forever Skills that we identified).

2. *What needs changing?* There is so much that needs changing. It needs people like you to change it. There has never been a time in history where you can make as much of a difference as now. So change something worth changing. Why not you? Why not now?

3. *What's unchanging?* Just as much is changing, so is much unchanging. People fundamentally do not change: our need to be loved, to laugh, cry, feel included, feel like we matter and that us being here makes a difference to the people we care for. None of that is going away.

We stated in the introduction that we aimed to launch a raft of calm into the sea of panic around change. Our mission is to help our readers, our leaders, our kids and even ourselves worry less and achieve more.

In other words, as Heraclitus advised us, we had better all get used to change being our constant companion in life.

What this leads us to conclude is this:

Firstly, that there are Forever Skills that are worth investing in. These will have value and provide us with success and influence no matter what the future brings. If we're going to remain relevant and future-proof ourselves, our children and our teams, we would do well to invest in them.

Secondly, that our greatest power ultimately lies within ourselves. Drawing on the wisdom of the Tolstoy maxim quoted at the beginning of this chapter, if we would change the world, we must first commit to changing ourselves. There is little use complaining about change or hoping it goes away, but preparation and a sense of resilience will always be critical assets, no matter where we choose to focus our energy and interest.

Lastly, and perhaps most importantly, the development of skills and capabilities, the need for constant and lifelong education and personal reinvention and development is in itself a Forever Skill.

CONCLUSION

Every epoch we traverse in the future will bring its own requirements in terms of skills and unique challenges to our existing values and conventions. If you hunger for certainty, then this is it, such as it is. Change is just how the system is meant to work ... we need to simply *deal with it!*

However, what this also means is that there is a great deal we can do personally to set ourselves, our organisations and our children up for success in the future.

The greatest Forever Skill we can pass on to future generations is a love of learning and a yearning for skills and capability.

This desire and need will remain relevant ... *forever.*

APPENDIX A
Looking back to look forward

Given we have termed the capabilities in this book 'Forever Skills', it seems likely that these skills informed our success and viability as a species throughout our history.

With that in mind, this appendix will detail some of what we found in terms of which skills have always been with us and how they might inform what matters today as well as what will matter tomorrow.

We divided human history into three not-so-neatly defined categories:

1. The Ancient World

2. Recent(ish) History

3. The Modern World (the world we occupy in the early twenty-first century).

The goal of this exercise, as with all of the research we've conducted, was to identify patterns and trends, and to isolate those skills that have proven to be evergreen and a consistent asset to those who wield them.

One of our key finds has been that often the words different cultures and industries use to describe certain skills or traits have varied. In fact, the variation in definitions of skills and the breadth of these definitions appears to be incredibly important. In this appendix, we've chosen to use the words selected by historians, archaeologists and sociologists to describe the daily lives and work skills of the cultures and times they have explored.

In the interest of 'utility over completeness' in our research, we focused on cultures that were either significantly successful or at least powerfully influential in their own time. We also considered that of those whose impact is still shaping the modern world today. While it would be nice to assess the work practices of the whole of human history, that is beyond the purpose and scope of this book.

IT ALL BEGAN QUITE A LONG TIME AGO ... IN THE ANCIENT WORLD

Our exploration of the ancient world has, to be frank, not been exhaustive.

One of the issues we faced that might bias this path of enquiry is the necessity for those cultures to have kept adequate written, or at least well-shared oral, records of daily life. This is critical so that we might reasonably draw some conclusions about the skills that played a part in their daily lives, their success and their evolution.

Included in our consideration have been:

- Indigenous cultures from around the world (including Australia, Africa and the Americas)
- Ancient Egypt
- Ancient Persia
- Ancient Mesopotamia
- Ancient India
- Ancient Greece
- the Roman Empire
- the empires of China and Japan.

As we had anticipated, there was a significant amount of alignment and duplication of skills from around the world. There are just some things we all have to deal with, no matter what postal or zip code we're born into.

A lot of this is drawn from the research of archaeologists, sociologists and historians, however the essential functions of human life are not terribly surprising.

The Ancient Chinese divided the working classes into four:

1. the *Shi* grouping was made up of scholars

2. the *Nong* were farmers and those engaged in food production

3. the *Gong* added meaning to life through art

4. the *Shang* were the merchant classes.

Like most ancient societies, social class was very hierarchical, with the four hierarchies listed in the order of their social importance.

Scholars occupied the upper echelons of society, while merchants sat at the bottom and were the least respected. (It seems life has always been tough for small-business people and entrepreneurs.)

The rest of the ancient world, much like the Chinese, shared a hierarchical view of both the work that was performed and the skills required to do that work. The higher the level of perceived skill, the higher the class or caste.

One fact worth noting is that the ancient world also made some rather clear distinctions in terms of gender and work. Given the relatively recent nature of the sexual revolution and women's suffrage, this is hardly surprising.

For now, let's consider some of the skill requirements, roles and work responsibilities that we saw were in repeated demand throughout the ancient world:

- nobility — a grouping the ancient Greeks referred to as 'aristocrats' (a term we still use today)

- politicians — which in Ancient Rome consisted of Patricians and Plebeians (the latter is still used as a pejorative to describe the same kinds of people today)

- priests and moral authorities

- administrators — including lawyers, census takers, scribes, tax collectors, scholars and educators

- artists and entertainers (including entertainers of a more adult nature)
- builders — which included masons and carpenters
- soldiers — including both the professional military and what we would call conscripts today
- farmers — and others engaged in food and beverage production
- trades and crafts — such as metal workers and hairdressers
- merchants and shopkeepers.

What emerged most commonly was that survival skills, such as food production, water gathering and the provision of shelter, were critical in every society. But noticeably, even in the ancient world, other key considerations appear to have been ubiquitous across all cultures:

- the need for safety and control — via a military force, moral authority and government bureaucracy
- a desire for connection, creativity, communication, recreation and mental stimulation — through the arts and entertainment
- the capacity to make the wheels of commerce turn — provided by the merchant classes, the trades and administrators and tax collectors.

While the skills and terminology varied from one culture to the next, what was universal was the function, role or value that was provided no matter where these very different cultures sat geographically, politically or chronologically.

But do these skills or characteristics transfer across history? Do they evolve? Or do they fall into disuse?

RECENT(ISH) HISTORY

In terms of recent history, we focused quite deliberately on Europe's Renaissance, the Industrial Revolution, the rise of the US economy post–World War II and the increased influence of Asian economies towards the end of the twentieth century.

As always, our guiding focus has been a bias towards the success and impact of cultures, regions and belief systems that exerted influence throughout the world in their time and beyond.

Perhaps most interesting in this period is the fact that we have, in a relatively short period of time, traversed multiple epochs, or technological ages. We first moved from the agrarian age to the agricultural, then into the age of enlightenment, followed by the first industrial revolution, into the information age and then to the early digital revolution we're still navigating today.

This unprecedented rate of acceleration in change provides a time lapse of history where we can, in a very short period of time, see skills, abilities, jobs and roles come into and out of favour, and also observe those that survived or evolved during the process.

Perhaps the most notable shift is a geographic one. This affects us at both a macro and micro level.

Large-scale migration was a defining feature of the eighteenth, nineteenth and twentieth centuries. This has largely been informed by Europe's colonisation of the 'New World', Asian and African migration and relocation, and the personal mobility we have enjoyed as a result of technological advances in transport.

Many of these migratory practices have been controversial, to say the least, as both slavery and conquest have displaced, removed and transported many human beings against their will.

We've also tended to be distracted by the macro nature of migration over the micro, by discussions of national demography and population composition. What has often been overlooked in the migration conversation of the late nineteenth and early twentieth centuries, which is perhaps even more impactful, is the migration from rural regions to urban areas.

THE FOUR INDUSTRIAL REVOLUTIONS

The First Industrial Revolution shaped the eighteenth and nineteenth centuries across Europe and North America. This was a time when mostly agrarian, rural communities became industrial and more urbanised.

This significantly informed the way we educate children and workers in the modern world, with many of our educational practices finding their origins in places like the 'Black Country' in the West Midlands of the UK. (So named because they became the smoky industrial powerhouse of Great Britain at the time.)

This revolution radically changed the mining, iron and textile industries and, along with the development of the steam engine, drove significant advances in technology accompanied by extraordinary disruption to both social and demographic conventions.

The Second Industrial Revolution is usually referred to as taking place between the late 1800s and the beginning of World War I. It was a period that is perhaps most influenced by humanity's use of what was at the time 'alternative energy'.

Fuel sources such as oil and electricity facilitated a shift from what were predominantly mechanical innovations to technologies that might be considered icons of the modern world. This included things such as the telephone, light bulbs and recording devices as well as the internal combustion engine, which led to the possibility of flight and widespread 'horseless' transportation for individuals and urban populations.

In the same way the First and Second industrial revolutions saw a shift from the mechanical to the electrical, the Third Industrial Revolution saw the advancement from analogue electronic technology and mechanical devices to the digital technology that is so ubiquitous today. This era is far more recent and has its origins in the 1980s. It was informed by changes in personal computing, internet accessibility and information and communications technology (ICT).

Of course, a reasonable argument might be made that we are still figuring out the changes wrought by the Third Industrial Revolution, although people like Professor Klaus Schwab, founder of the World Economic Forum and author of *The Fourth Industrial Revolution*, argue that a significant tipping point has again been passed as we move towards the 'internet of things'.

This takes us into a new phase of technology that people like Google's in-house futurist Ray Kurzweil would call 'The Singularity', the convergence of the digital and biological worlds.

This Fourth Industrial Revolution is being shaped by the new ways in which technology might become embedded within our societies and even incorporated on or inside the human body. It is defined by emerging technological breakthroughs in a number of fields including robotics, artificial intelligence, nanotechnology, quantum computing, biotechnology, the internet of things, 3D printing and autonomous vehicles.

On the back of Schwab's theories about the Fourth Industrial Revolution, the World Economic Forum also outlined the shifts in skills that they believed would inform the then future (2020) in their Future of Jobs Report published in 2015. The top ten skills saw significant shifts predicted to take place in the five intervening years, as shown in table A.1.

Table A.1 the top 10 skills, 2015 versus 2020

TOP 10 SKILLS IN 2015	TOP 10 SKILLS IN 2020
1. Complex problem solving	1. Complex problem solving
2. Coordinating with others	2. Critical thinking
3. People management	3. Creativity
4. Critical thinking	4. People management
5. Negotiation	5. Coordinating with others
6. Quality control	6. Emotional intelligence
7. Service orientation	7. Judgement and decision making
8. Judgement and decision making	8. Service orientation
9. Active listening	9. Negotiation
10. Creativity	10. Cognitive flexibility

Source: Future of Jobs Report, World Economic Forum

This latest revolution is defined by what are often considered to be the most frightening technological changes we have faced as a species.

This is partly because it's actually difficult for us to project ourselves into the mindset of those who lived in the past and truly empathise with what agricultural labourers might have experienced as they abandoned their subsistence farms and tried to navigate the First Industrial Revolution in the late eighteenth century. But it's also uniquely challenging because these changes point to a world where, for the very first time, the very purpose and necessity of human beings is being questioned.

Jobs, skills and roles that we had once thought of as being eternally useful might fade from history, with some futurists (finding a pedigree in the work of Richard Buckminster 'Bucky' Fuller) suggesting that full employment within a society might no longer be a relevant social goal or even economically necessary.

This creates immense social angst and confusion as it rocks the very foundations we have built our civilisations on. We stand at the precipice of a future where we may need to reset our thinking about how resources and wealth are distributed and, just as importantly, how we apportion and spend our time.

GENDER AND GEOGRAPHIC DIFFERENCES AND SIMILARITIES

One of the more controversial aspects of this exploration of history is the significant challenges and inequalities that exist in different eras and geographies regarding different genders and ethnicities.

This, of course, presented its own set of issues for us in writing this book. For example, in analysing the skills and work practices of the past, it's hard to ignore the biases and injustices of slavery, segregation and the hard lines that have been drawn between the roles of different genders throughout history.

We decided it is not in the scope of this book to judge the sins and prejudices of the past. Frankly, this is far too short a book to address problems of that scale and significance in any great detail.

We have, however, endeavoured to keep our observations as relevant to the modern world as we can and, in doing so, keep our descriptions as gender neutral and geo-politically sensitive as possible.

APPENDIX B
Today's workplace trends

It turns out 'here today' doesn't always mean 'gone tomorrow'.

However, if we were asked to choose a word to critique the modern world, it would be hard to go past the word 'disposable'. Where once we were obsessed with how well something was made or the quality of the stitching, the woodwork or the engineering, today our focus is much more on price and convenience.

In fact 'disposable' is a term that has been used to describe the Western world's entire economic outlook, from our wastefulness of resources to our short-term attention spans and our hyper-consumption.

And there's plenty of evidence for this criticism. We squander resources thoughtlessly: our energy consumption is polluting the planet and becoming economically unsustainable, our 'single use' attitude is creating land 'over-fill' (and islands of plastic in the oceans) as well undermining craft and expertise. Even human beings have come to be treated as commodities that are useful right up until the point that they're not.

This has also informed our thinking around work and life skills. We tend to only think about skills as being trend-based and time-defined and -limited, but there is reason to think that this might not be the case.

In fact there is a plethora of research into the skills that will matter going forward, what the future of work will look like and where we should invest our education dollar for ourselves and our children.

Many of these studies from the worlds of academia, professional services, human resources and recruitment have helped shape much of the direction our own research took. What's also immediately apparent from the quantity of this research is how much passion and interest this field of enquiry stimulates.

However, a critical distinction between the work of these academics, recruiters and consultants and our own is one of intent. While they have sought to identify what is new, what will change, what we'll need to add to the repertoire of human ability, we have focused primarily on what will remain and be a constant in this world of change.

Many of these 'new skills' are no doubt incredibly useful for those looking to read the direction that the winds of change are blowing in; however, some and perhaps most of these skills might be considered temporary and transient; what we call 'Age-Based Intelligence'.

In other words, they belong to a particular age, epoch or era of history.

For example, an ability to work a forge was probably incredibly useful during the iron age, but perhaps less so now that 3D printing and automation have forever changed how we shape and mould metal (and even the elements that such metal comprises).

However, just as an understanding of past and present work trends is incredibly important, so too is exploring what other experts are looking at now and into the future.

CURRENT TRENDS AND FUTURE FOCUS

To better understand the current state of play in the field of skills development and where future attention might be focused, we first looked at what research into the future of work was already out there. And there's plenty of it.

This research into future skills pretty much boils down to four areas of interest (or at least these were the ones that most piqued *our* interest):

1. *Academic funding.* Where are we looking?
2. *HR focus.* Who are we looking for?
3. *Workplace shifts.* What are we buying?
4. *Future of work research.* What are we investing in?

These are simply what we believe are the most obvious choices given their proximity to the issue itself. Some of the studies, white papers and articles that informed our initial research included:

- Accenture's 'Harnessing Revolution — Creating the Future Workforce' by Ellyn Shook & Mark Knickrehm (2017)

- Adobe's 'The Future of Work' (2018)

- *Australian Financial Review*'s 'Nothing Soft About the Soft Skills' by Mark Eggleton (2018)

- *Australian Financial Review*'s 'Technology to Augment Rather Than Replace' by Mark Eggleton (2018)

- Brookings' 'The Future of Work in Africa' by Amy Copley (2018)

- Ceda's 'Australia's Future Workforce' (2015)

- Cedefop's 'Future Skills Needs in Europe — Critical Labour Force Trends' (2016)

- Cognizant's 'The Work Ahead — The Future of Business and Jobs in Asia Pacific's Digital Economy' by Manish Bahl (2016)

- Corrs Chambers Westgarth's 'The Future of Work in the Asia–Pacific' by Professor Anthony Forsyth (2017)

- Council on Foreign Relations 'The Work Ahead' (2018)

- Deloitte South Africa's 'The Future of Work' by Valter Adáo (2018)

- Deloitte's 'Soft Skills for Business Success' (2018)

- Deloitte's 'The Future of the Workforce' by Jeff Schwartz, Josh Bersin, Juliet Bourke, Robert Danna, Madonna Jarraet, Angus Knowles-Cultler, Harvey Lewis & Bill Pelster (2016)

- Eco-Business's 'The Future of work in Developing Asia' by Ingrid van Wees (2018)

- Ericsson's 'The Next Generation Working Life — A Survival Guide' (2018)

- Ericsson's 'The Next Generation Working Life — From Workplace to exchange Place' (2013)

- EY's 'The Future of Work' (2018)

- EY's 'What if employment as we know it disappears tomorrow?' by Silvia Hernandez, Ulrike Hasbargen, Gerard Osei-Bonsu, Valentina Roselli & Regina Karner (2018)

- FastCompany's '5 Super Skills You Need for Jobs of the Future' by Stephanie Vozza (2018)

- Forbes Technology Council's '13 Top Tech Skills in High Demand for 2018' (2018)

- FYA's 'The New Work Mindset — 7 New Job Clusters to Help Young People Navigate the New Work Order' (2017)

- *Harvard Business Review's* 'The Future of You' by Tomas Chamorro-Premuzic (2013)

- Hays's '10 Recruitment Trends for 2018' (2018)

- Hays's 'Hotspots of Skills in Demand' (2018)

- International Labour Office's 'Technology Anxiety Past & Present' by David Autor & David Dorn (2013)

- International Labour Office's 'The Future of Work, Employment and Skills in Latin America and the Caribbean' by José Manuel Salazar-Xirinachs (2017)

- International Labour Organization's 'The Future of work — The Meaning and Value of Work in Europe' by Dominique Méda (October 2017)

- LinkedIn's 'The Most Promising and In-Demand Skills of 2018' (2018)

- McKinsey & Company's 'Digitally Enabled Automation and Artificial Intelligence' (2017)

- McKinsey & Company's 'Future of Work Report' (2018)

- MIT Technology Review's 'How is America Preparing for the Future of Work?' by Erin Winnick (2018)

- Monster.com's 'These 7 Work Skills Can Make You More Marketable to Employers' by Daniel Bortz (2018)

- My Business's 'Recruiters Most Sought-After Skills in 2018' (2018)

- Observer Research Foundation's 'The Future of Work in Asia' by Marc Saxer (2018)

- PwC's 'The Long View — How Will the Economic Order Change by 2050?' by John Hawksworth, Hannah Audino & Rob Clarry (2017)

- PwC's 'The Workforce of the Future — The Competitive Forces Shaping 2030' by Carol Stubbings (2018)

- Randstad's 'Six Workforce Trends to Dominate in 2018' (2017)

- RBC's 'Future Skills Report' (2018)

- The European Political Strategy Centre's 'The Future of Work' (2016)

- The World Economic Forum's 'The Future of Jobs and Skills in Africa — Preparing the Region for the Fourth Industrial Revolution' by Richard Samans & Saadia Zahdi (2017)

- Upwork's 'Future Workforce HR Report' (2018)

- Willis Towers Watson's 'Five Myths About the Future of Work' (2018)

- World Economic Forum's '2018 Economic Forum on Latin America' (2018)

- World Economic Forum's '8 Job Skills Every Company Will Be Hiring for in 2010' by Cadie Thompson (2016)

So what did we learn from all of this research? Again, as with our historical research, patterns began to emerge, some predictable, some less so. While much of the existing research focused on new technical skills such as robotics, engineering coding, artificial intelligence and the like, they were almost always augmented by skill sets that seemed familiar.

So while digital literacy might be seen as a pressing need based on the moment we're living in right now, so too were things such as communication skills, problem solving, creativity and commercial acumen. Even when the focus was purely on the future, the research pointed to the fact that much of what was already important would continue to be.

This absolutely mirrors the findings of our own research.

APPENDIX C
Ten years of work and research

One of the great privileges of the work we have done over the past decade, and even across the past 30 years if we're honest, is that we get the opportunity to work with different industries and professionals in different parts of the world almost every day of the year. In fact, there is scarcely an industry we haven't worked with.

The great advantage of having such a rich and diverse professional history is that we are privy to the macro trends that run across all industries, not just one small part of the professional world.

It has also allowed us to ask a huge cross-section of the global community the kinds of questions few get the opportunity to, and exposed us to the kind of in-confidence strategic information that, to be frank, should make it illegal for us to be able to trade in the stock market.

The nature of the work we now do, as corporate speakers and organisational trainers, also means we have the access and means to ask questions of hundreds and even thousands of people in different industries in a single moment and then collect the answers via digital technology such as live polling. This gives us access to huge sample sizes without having to make annoying cold calls and interrupt people's dinner time.

This means the very nature of our work is research-based, which gives us multiple methodologies through which we can find the truth that sits across categories, within industries as a whole and in the individuals who populate them.

These methodologies include:

- strategic conversations with leadership teams in virtually every industry sector and category

- engaging with thousands of individuals via social media, in corporate workshops and in-audience conference surveys using digital and good old-fashioned analogue technology (hands up!)

- over 100 interviews with various experts in their fields from around the world.

So how did we approach this concept of predicting what will make it into the future?

Firstly, we looked at identifying the critical industry sectors to research. Now, there are many lists segmenting industry categories and just as many metrics for applying these distinctions. So we gathered lists from international industry sector groups, from HR consultancies, leadership development organisations and professional services firms, including PwC, who list the industry sectors like this:

- agribusiness
- asset and wealth management
- banking and finance
- construction and transportation
- defence
- education
- energy (oil and gas)
- entertainment and media
- financial services
- government
- healthcare
- infrastructure
- insurance
- mining

- power and utilities
- real estate
- retail
- technology.

We then created a list of experts and industry influencers from each of these categories to interview.

What was critical in this process was the need for diversity, not because it was the 'right' thing to do, but because it afforded us more points of view from which to explore our central question.

This meant leaning pretty heavily on our international network to get a mix of opinions within different economic models, cultural expectations, gender mixes, industry experience and educational backgrounds.

We then made sure that our research methodology was equally broad.

QUANT, QUAL AND QUESTIONS

Once we had established an industry framework that was broad enough to capture macro trends, and populated it with a mix of business leaders, celebrities, sportspeople, entrepreneurs and thought leaders, we wanted to gather the information in different ways so that we could see what people were thinking as a whole and then drill down into what that meant for them and their industry specifically.

We started with qualitative research, distributing online surveys through platforms such as LinkedIn and Facebook that allowed us to target particular industry and interest groups as well as specific geographies and targeted demographics.

We then added these kinds of surveys into our keynote speaking and training workshops, using live digital surveys to capture hundreds of responses at a time.

Our initial surveys were quite high-level and relatively simple. We simply offered participants different lists of skills and asked them to choose which three they believed would be the most important in the future, ranked in order.

Later, we added more specificity to our surveys such as, 'Which do you think will be the most important *leadership* skills in the future?' Followed by *problem solving* skills, *people management* skills, *self-development* skills and so on. These distinctions were informed by our initial surveys as being areas of keen interest, with each new survey being informed in some way by the one that preceded it.

The results we gathered were, to be honest, *depressingly* predictable.

If you've spent any time in the corporate, government or organisational world in the past five years, you could probably guess which skills trended the highest.

However, while the quant data didn't vary much from our initial hypothesis, the qualitative research was rather more revealing.

It turns out that while many of us are using the same generic language to describe groups of skills and capabilities, what we mean by those words can be radically different.

Our qualitative research, which consisted of sitting with over 100 experts for at least an hour, generated responses and insights that even they hadn't expected.

The style of interview we chose was informed by seven simple questions. However, we almost never stuck to the script and this allowed us to more organically explore wherever the conversation might take us. In other words, our questions were a starting point rather than a limitation.

The questions we asked included:

- What three skills have been most important to you and your success throughout your career?

- What do you believe the most important life and work skills are right now in your field or industry?

- What do you think the most important life and work skills in the future will be?

- Which skills are likely to be outsourced overseas or automated by robotics and artificial intelligence? Which skills do you think cannot be outsourced or automated?

- Where are you investing your time and money for your education? Or for your children's education?

- What do you believe are the top three skills critical to any kind of success?

- What will always be important or valuable to the people, clients, customers or constituents that you serve in your industry?

So what did we learn?

LANGUAGE MATTERS ... A LOT

Perhaps unsurprisingly, language is particularly important.

As we write this particular appendix we are sitting in a hotel restaurant in Amsterdam surrounded by other businesspeople chattering away in German, Mandarin, French and of course Dutch. These are only the languages we can personally identify over the buzz of caffeinated conversation that is to be found in hotels all around the world.

However, when we speak of language in the context of this book, we're not so much referring to languages native to particular nations or ethnicities; we're referring to the descriptors designated to particular skills as well as the jargon and dialects that particular industry categories and cultures have a preference for.

It turns out that words and phrases such as 'leadership', 'resilience', 'creativity' and 'people skills' mean a myriad different things to different people.

'Leadership', for instance, might be described by one expert in their field as people management; another may assert that it is vision-setting and strategic execution; still another might describe a command-and-control methodology, while others articulate a more laissez-faire approach to engaging people in the pursuit of a common cause.

Likewise, we found that 'resilience' can mean everything from a sense of mindfulness or 'centredness' with regard to change, to a capacity to create new possibilities as others faded or eroded. It was even (rather less generously) described as an ability to beat yourself into emotional stoicism and internalise a sense of, 'Suck it up precious'.

Of course, none of these particular definitions might be considered 'the' truth but merely aspects of truth that we need to unravel and piece together so that a complete picture of these skills might be assembled.

So, it is worth explaining our definitions of the above distinctions and how they fit with those of the people we spoke to.

SKILLS VS TRAITS VS ROLES VS VALUES

So what is the difference between doing, being and delivering? In other words, is a skill something you do? A trait something you have intrinsically? And a role or value a framework you act within or else something you deliver? Or are they all interchangeable?

Another distinction that some of the experts we interviewed made was between skills and capabilities. Some argued that skills seemed to be more short-lived and functional, whereas a capability might be more associated with a longer term development. Others suggested that a capability might simply indicate a talent, whereas a skill required work and dedication.

Quite the dilemma!

This has been one of the most persistent questions that our research presented and has led to some interesting distinctions about what a skill actually is.

So which is the best frame to use?

For our purposes, we defined a skill as something that may be learned, taught or else developed through purposeful practice. The outcome of which must certainly be some form of value, either economic, social or recreational.

We also decided to stick with 'skills' as it is a word that connotes both utility and practicality while seeming to be the most universally understood in the context of education, training and personal development.

However, in light of the above, please don't let our choice of language get in the way of your own sense of meaning, and do feel free to editorialise in your heads if you are so inclined.

MACRO TRENDS AND INDUSTRY INSIGHTS

Our primary filter for the research we conducted was the desire for pattern recognition. Rather than simply narrowing down to a specific word or phrase, we were more interested in identifying the meaning behind such words and whether they were repeated across industries, cultures and time.

Many of the macro trends that emerged seemed to vary insignificantly across industries and territories, with a few specific exceptions. However, when we dug into specific genres of skills, new distinctions emerged.

For instance, retailers in the United States, miners in Australia and bankers in Europe might all consider 'emotional intelligence' and 'problem solving' to be key skills at a macro level. However, what each of these meant by 'problem solving' at a more granular definition was very informative.

After we conducted multiple surveys, polls and interviews across industries, we decided to switch our research from broad, single-word statements that might be generically understood to looking to codify specific clusters of skills.

For example, what did 'problem solving' (a particularly broad skill description) actually require? Was it creativity? Strategy? Critical thinking? Design skills? Behavioural science? The answer was usually a mix of all of these skills but in different measures under different circumstances.

This is perhaps one of the most critical points we will make in this book. Through all of our education in school, college or university, we have been trained to think of skills and intelligence as being partitioned along particular lines. Maths usually sits with science, art with drama, social sciences with languages and so on.

However, we have come to realise that a more useful frame is to consider groups of skills as clusters that are inevitably interconnected. While it may be convenient to consider one or two in isolation, it's also worth filtering the connections between all skills.

In many ways, this echoes some of Dan Pink's thinking around 'symphony' in his 2005 book *A Whole New Mind*, but it also draws on the richness of thinking that defined the 'renaissance' minds we still revere today.

Leonardo da Vinci is perhaps the most notable example of this. Today he is most known for his skills as a portrait artist, but he was also reported to have been incredibly physically fit, a gifted musician, an inventor, engineer, architect and weapons designer.

While identifying the Forever Skills, this capacity to orchestrate multiple skills or to think of skills in terms of 'symphony', coordinated and harmonised, was also revealed as being incredibly important.

In other words, when we think of 'Forever Skills' as a concept, we need to understand that they are skills, plural, and interconnected.

THE AUTHORS

Kieran Flanagan is a global thought leader in commercial creativity and Dan Gregory is an expert in behavioural strategy. Together they are the co-founders of The Impossible Institute™ — a strategic think tank founded to re-imagine the way we think, lead, navigate change and create success.

They are the strategic and creative team behind the most successful new product launch in Australian history, have helped entrepreneurs build internationally successful businesses and worked with some of the world's most influential organisations: developing communication and marketing strategies for Coca-Cola; driving innovation and product design for Unilever; delivering leadership development for the Australian Navy and banks based in Asia; building teamwork in global tech giants and C-suite executives in the United States, as well as facilitating social-change strategies for the United Nations in Singapore and NGOs in Australia.

Voted in the 'top 25 C-Suite Speakers to watch' by Meetings & Conventions USA, they combine business acumen with a rapier wit and rare human insight gained while working on the US and UK stand-up comedy circuits — skills put to great use in front of millions of viewers on ABC TV's *Gruen* franchise and Channel 7's *Masters of Spin* and as regular contributors to *Success* and *The CEO Magazine* in the United States.

www.TheImpossibleInstitute.com

@TheImpossibleIn

@ThinkKieranF

@DanGregoryCo

THE PODCAST

Want to know more about the *Forever Skills* in this book?
Listen to the companion podcast at FOREVERSKILLS.COM

INDEX